George Wither

The Hymns and Songs of the Church

With an Introduction by Edward Farr

George Wither

The Hymns and Songs of the Church
With an Introduction by Edward Farr

ISBN/EAN: 9783744767071

Printed in Europe, USA, Canada, Australia, Japan

Cover: Foto ©Lupo / pixelio.de

More available books at **www.hansebooks.com**

Library of Old Authors.

Loe this is he whose infant Muse begann
To braue the World before yeares stil'd him Man;
Though praise be sleight & scornes to make his Rymes
Begg fauors or opinion of the Tymes,
Yet few by good men haue bine more approu'd
None so vnseene, so generally lou'd

S. T. I.

Non pictoris opus fuit hoc sed pectoris, Vnde
Diuinæ in Tabulam mentis imago fuit

J. W.

HYMNS AND SONGS OF THE CHURCH

BY GEORGE WITHER.

WITH AN INTRODUCTION BY

EDWARD FARR.

LONDON:
REEVES & TURNER,
5, WELLINGTON STREET, STRAND, W.C.
1895.

INTRODUCTION.

AMONG the numerous poets of the sixteenth and seventeenth centuries there is scarcely a name more worthy of honour than that of George Wither.

Some writers have, indeed pronounced Wither a fanatical rhymer and an intemperate Puritan. Such was the judgment of Ritson, Heylin, Dryden, Swift and Pope: all writers of undoubted talent, but whose criticism and taste must have been governed by prejudice. In the "neglected leaves" of Wither, Dr. Southey discerned "felicity of expression;" "tenderness of feeling;" and "elevation of mind;" and Sir Egerton Brydges, Mr. Park, Mr. Willmott, and that truly Christian poet and critic, James Montgomery, have all borne testimony to Wither's merits. The cloud which obscured his merits as a poet, arose from his mingling in the political warfare of the turbulent period in which he lived.

Sir Egerton Brydges in his Restituta has thus given the pedigree of the poet.

"Thomas Wither of the County of Lancaster, Esq., left three sons.

"Robert Wither, third son, came to Manydowne in Hampshire, and there lived, leaving issue.

"Thomas Wither, of Manydowne, who married Joane, daughter and heir of Richard Mason of Lydmonton in Hampshire, and had three sons, John, Thomas, and Richard.

"John, eldest son, of Manydowne who married Ann daughter of—Ayliffe of Skeynes in Hampshire, had three sons, John, Richard and George (which last married Avelyn, daughter of John Shank, and had Gilbert, Thomas, John and Reginald; and the said Gilbert was father of George, William, Reginald and Henry.)

"Richard Wither, second son of John Wither and Ann Ayliffe, was of Manydowne, and married a daughter of William Poynter of Whitchurch in Hampshire, by whom he had four sons, John, George, (*father of the poet*) Otho and Ferdinando,

"John Wither of Manydowne, eldest son, married Jane, daughter of John Love of Basing in Hampshire, and had five sons, William, Anthony, John, James, and Richard. William eldest son, was of Manydowne, and married Susan, daughter of Paul Risley of Chetwood in Buckinghamshire, and had issue, John, Paul, and Susan.

"George Wither (second son of Richard Wither by the daughter of—Poynter) had issue three sons, viz., George Wither the poet, James Wither, and Anthony Wither.

In most of Wither's poems something of his private history may be collected. The date of his birth even is better substantiated by his verse than by the baptismal Register. Aubrey and Anthony Wood state that he was born in 1588; others authors assert that the poet was born in

1590. His verse settles the question in favour of Wood and Aubrey. In a pamphlet entitled "Salt upon Salt," written and published in 1658 he writes :—

> When I began to know the world and men,
> I made records of what I found it then,
> Continuing even since to take good heed
> How they stood still, went back, or did proceed:
> Till of my scale of time ascending heaven
> The round I stand in maketh ten times seven.

"Ten times seven" or seventy years, fixes the date of his birth in 1588.

The poet received his early education in the village of Colemore, under one John Greaves, a schoolmaster of some celebrity. The tutor evidently gained the love of his pupil, for he is noticed in the poet's epigrams in this touching language :—

> If ever I do wish I may be rich
> (As oft perhaps such idle breath I spend),
> I do it not for anything so much,
> As to have wherewithal to pay my friend ;
> For trust me there is nothing grieves me more
> Than this, that I should still much kindness take,
> And have a fortune to my mind so poor;
> That though I would amends I cannot make ;
> Yet to be still as thankful as I may,
> (Sith my estate no better means afford)
> What I indeed receive, I do repay
> In willingness, in thanks, and gentle words.

The father of the poet appears to have enjoyed considerable affluence, for alluding to his juvenile years, Wither, in a poem entitled Britain's Remembrancer, writes :—

> When daily I on change of dainties fed,
> Lodged night by night upon an easy bed,
> In lordly chambers and had wherewithall
> Attendants forwarder than I to call,

> Who brought me all things needful; when at hand
> Hounds, hawks and horses were at my command,
> Then chose I did my walks on hills or vallies
> In groves, near springs, or in sweet garden allies,
> Reposing either in a natural shade
> Or in neat harbours which by hands were made,
> Where I might have required without denial,
> The lute, the organ or deepsounding viol,
> To cheer my spirits; with what else beside
> Was pleasant, when my friends did thus provide
> Without my cost or labour.

From the village school of Colemore Wither was sent to Magdalen College, Oxford, and it was here that his poetical talents were first developed. Before he left the school of Greaves he had become acquainted with " Lilly's Latin " and " Camden's Greek," but at the University he seems to have neglected classical learning, and to have devoted his powers to the Muses, until his kind old tutor, "by his good persuasion," again brought him to a love of what he had been taught. Then after Cynthia "had six times lost her borrowed light," he again " drank at Aristotle's well."

It was while Wither was redevoting his attention to classical studies and when he had been at Oxford about two years, and was beginning to love a college life, that the change in his father's temporal circumstances seems to have taken place, for he was suddenly removed from the University and taken home " to hold the plough." He alludes thus touchingly to this change in " Abuses Whipt and Stript :"—

> But now ensues the worst—I setting foot
> And thus digesting learning's bitter root,
> Ready to taste the fruit; then when I thought
> I should a calling in that place have sought,
> I found that I for other ends ordain'd
> Was from that course perforce to be constrain'd.

INTRODUCTION.

If the plough had a charm for Cincinnatus, not so had it for Wither. According to Aubrey he returned in discontent to the " beechy shadows of Brentworth ;" and his sojourn at home was more embittered by officious friends, who were constantly urging his relations to apprentice him to some trade. But the mind of Wither was not to be cast down. When only eighteen years of age he made his way to London of his own accord, there to seek his fortune. Shortly after his arrival in the metropolis, he entered himself of Lincoln's Inn, where he appears to have formed an acquaintance with the pastoral poet, William Brown, who belonged to the Inner Temple. This seems to have been the turning point in his history. Anthony Wood says that hanging after things more smooth and delightful than the law, he did at length make himself known to the world by certain specimens of his poetry, which being dispersed in several hands, he became shortly after a public author.

The poetical works of George Wither are numerous. Most of them are of a secular character, but interspersed throughout his writings are beautiful passages indicating the mind of a Christian. There is the fine gold of Christian thought even in "Abuses Stript and Whipt," a satire of the most galling nature; and in " Prince Henry's Obsequies," "Epithalamia," or "Nuptial Poems," the "Shepherd's Hunting," the "Motto," "Fair Virtue," the "Remembrancer," and the "Emblems," there are lines on almost every page which reflect a hallowed light over much that is unworthy of a Christian poet.

In his earlier years of authorship Wither

appears to have obtained the semblance of court favour. But the favour of courts is proverbially fickle, and so Wither found. His expectations of preferment were not realised, and being unable to procure preferment, he applied himself to watching the vices of the times. These vices were abundant, and in his "Abuses Stript and Whipt," he exposed them unsparingly. Never did satirist write with more thrilling effect, but the chief result of his exertions to mend the public morals was his committal to the Marshalsea prison. What sufferings he there endured he thus describes in the "Scholar's Purgatory:"—

"All my apparent good intentions were so mistaken by the aggravation of some ill affected towards my endeavours, that I was shut up from the society of mankind, and as one unworthy the compassion vouchsafed to thieves and murderers, was neither permitted the use of my pen, the access or sight of acquaintance, the allowances usually afforded other close prisoners, nor means to send for necessaries befitting my present condition: by which means I was for many days compelled to feed on nothing but the coarsest bread, and sometimes locked up four-and-twenty hours together, without so much as a drop of water to cool my tongue: and being at the same time in one of the grossest extremities of dullness that was ever inflicted upon my body, the help both of physician and apothecary was uncivilly denied me. So that if God had not, by resolutions of the mind which he infused into me, extraordinarily enabled me to wrestle with those and such other afflictions as I was then exercised withall,

I had been dangerously and lastingly overcome. But of these usages I complain not; he that made me, made me strong enough to despise them."

But Wither did not so quietly endure his incarceration as these last sentences would lead us to suppose. His "Shepherds Hunting" was written in the Marshalsea, which, although it is a pastoral poem of great beauty, yet contains some passages burning with indignation against his persecutors. But his indignation is more clearly seen in a satire which he addressed to King James. In this satire he writes:—

> Did I not know a great man's power and might
> In spite of innocence can smother right,
> Colour his villanies to get esteem,
> And make the honest man the villain seem.
> I know it, and the world doth know 'tis true,
> Yet I protest if such a man I knew,
> That might my country prejudice or thee
> Were he the greatest or the proudest he,
> That breathes this day; if so it might be found
> That any good to either might redound,
> I unappalled, dare in such a case
> Rip up his foulest crimes before his face,
> Thou for my labour I was sure to drop
> Into the mouth of ruin without hope.

This Satire was addressed to the King in 1614 and it has been asserted that his liberation from prison was attributable to its influence. It would rather appear from some lines in one of his Emblems, that his release was owing to the friendly interposition of the Earl of Pembroke. He writes that this friend—

> found such means and place
> To bring and reconcile me to his grace,

> That therewithall his majesty bestow'd
> A gift upon me which his bounty show'd
> And had enrich'd me if what was intended
> Had not by othersome been ill befriended.

The gift alluded to in these lines was a patent for his Hymns and Songs of the Church. This is the work we lay before our readers, and it may be safely asserted that none of Wither's works possess greater interest.

The King's patent bears date the 17th of February, 1622-3. It reads thus:—"James by the Grace of God. To all and singular printers, booksellers. Whereas, our well-beloved subject George Wither, gentleman, by his great industry and diligent study has gathered and composed a book, entitled Hymns and Songs of the Church, by him faithfully and briefly translated into lyric verse, which said book being esteemed worthy and profitable to be inserted in convenient manner and due place into every English Psalm book in metre. We give and grant full and free license, power and privilege unto the said George Wither, his executors and assigns, only to imprint or cause to be imprinted, for the term of fifty and one years, etc. Witness our self at Westminster the 17th day of February." Reg. 20—1622-3.

The origin of the privilege granted by King James have thus been explained by Wither:—

"For before I had license to come abroad again into the world, I was forced to pay expenses so far beyond my ability that ere I could be clearly discharged, I was left many pounds worse than nothing and to enjoy the name of liberty, was cast into a greater bondage than before. Wherefore coming abroad again into the world, accompanied thither with those affections which are natural to most men, I was loth (if it might conveniently be prevented) either to sink below my rank, or to live at the mercy of a creditor. And, therefore, having none of those helps, or trades, or shifts which many others have to relieve themselves withall, I humbly petitioned the King's most excellent Majesty (not to be supplied at his, or by any projectment to the oppression of his people) but that according to the laws of Nature, I might enjoy the benefits of my own labours, by virtue of his royal privilege. His Majesty vouchsafed my reasonable request with addition of voluntary favours beyond my own desire."

But the publication of the Hymns and Songs of the Church brought no profit to their author. The work did not, it is true, like " Abuses Stript and Whipt," have the effect of casting him into the Marshalsea prison, but it not only failed to produce him the profit he so much needed and desired, but it raised against him a powerful body of active and malignant enemies in the Company of Stationers, who considered their own privileges invaded by the patent the King had granted to Wither. The result of the publication of the Hymns and Songs is related in the before mentioned curious prose tract entitled " The Scholar's Purgatory," which Wither issued in 1624. This tract was addressed to Archbishop Abbott and the other bishops of the Convocation, in vindication of the patent. The following copious extract from it is deeply interesting, as relating to the poetical pages of this volume :—

" With a good purpose, I began and finished those Hymns and Songs, which make up the book called, the HYMNS AND SONGS OF THE CHURCH. So named, not for that I would have them accounted part of our Liturgy, as I have delivered to his Majesty in my Epistle; but because they do for the most part treat of such particulars as concern the whole Church of God. And this is that Book, for which his Majesty vouchsafed me the privilege before mentioned, and which he piously and graciously commanded to be annexed to the *Singing Psalms*, that it might be the more generally and more conveniently divulged among his subjects, for their instruction.

"And indeed, by that means, these poor people, whose pastors suffer them, or cause them to be misinformed concerning that point, shall carry about with them, in their most usual book, what may at one time or other open their understandings, to perceive their error.

"This is that Book, for which I, ever worst used for my best intentions, suffer more than for all my former indiscretions; and for which I have received those affronts, that may well be ranked among my greatest injuries; notwithstanding it had besides the ordinary allowance of authority, the particular approbation and commendation both of the King himself, and of many the Members of this most reverend Convocation.

"Yea, this is that Book, for which the Commonwealth of Stationers, a tyranny unheard of in former ages, desire to make me as odious, as if I had employed my whole study to the oppression of this weal public, or to the subversion of religion: and for which they have pursued me with such violence and clamour, as hath seldom or never been exampled in any cause.

* * * *

" Some give out that my Book contains nothing but a few needless Songs; which I composed, and got privilege by Patent, merely for my private benefit, to the oppression of the Commonwealth.

" Some discourage those that come to buy the Book; otherwhiles denying that it is to be had; and otherwhile peremptorily protesting against the selling of it; or disgracefully telling such as enquire after the same, that the book is ridiculous; and that it better befitted me to meddle with my Poetry than to be tampering with Divinity; with such like other words of contempt.

" Other some there be, who dare aver that my Lord's Grace of Canterbury, with many of the Bishops and best Divines, do much dislike and oppose the said HYMNS.

" Others again buzz in the people's ears, that the Hymns for the observable times are Popish, and tending to the maintenance of superstition.

" And some there be among them, who in such terms of ribaldry, as no Stews can go beyond them, blasphemingly affirm, that the CANTICLES are obscene, and not fit to be divulged in song or verse.

"Yea, many other objections they make, and cast out diverse aspersions, as well upon the Author, as on his Book, to bring both into contempt.

* * * *

" To keep myself the closer to that, which shall be pertinent to this apology, I will make these particular objections my themes, which I have repeated: nor will I bring any other authorities to make good my defence than the true relations of what hath been done, and such plain arguments as mine own reason shall be able to frame. For, if this discourse come to the view of your Reverences only, you well enough know what the records of antiquity can afford to these purposes. And if it happen among those only of mean capacity, such plain expressions, as I purpose to use, will acquire most credit among them.

"And, first, whereas they give out that my *Hymns* are needless; they do not only by there contemn and slight my pains, but lay imputation upon the wisdom of the Holy Ghost also. For a great part of them are parcels of the Canonical Scriptures; originally *Song*. And to say, any fragment thereof were needless, is, in effect, to diminish from God's words, upon which follows a heavy curse.

"God deserves every day to be praised of us for delivering his Church, by the overthrow of Pharoah in the Red Sea, as much as he did in the very moment of their deliverance. And the Song of Moses, then used, doth in every particular, as properly concern every Christian congregation, as it did the Jews themselves upon that occasion. For God's mercy shewed to us in our baptism, and the spiritual overthrow of the Devil, pursuing us with an host of sins and temptations, is, in mine opinion, more effectually expressed to a spiritual understanding by apprehending the actions and circumstances of that temporal deliverance, than it could be by the power of any words, or by any other ordinary means; except by contemplating, of that most excellent material object, the Sacrament of Baptism itself, of which the other was but a type.

INTRODUCTION. xvii

"In like manner, all the other *Canonical Hymns* do admirably help towards God's everlasting mercies, and for illustrating those particular mysteries of our Christian Faith, which they did typically and prophetically foreshow. Yea, they are part of the Prophetical Witness, as the Hymns of the New Testament are part of the Evangelical Witness, of our interest in Christ Jesus. And, verily, the late neglect of their application in our Christian mysteries hath not only much injured one of the two great witnesses of our salvation, but given occasion also, that many unsound professors have corrupted them, even to the bringing in of diverse Jewish and Talmudical fancies, to the fearful distraction of weak people.

"But, were not those Hymns necessary in respect of the variety of their arguments, yet the variety of expression were somewhat needful, although the matter were the same. For, as the several dressings of one sort of meat make it diversely agreeable to the palates and stomachs of men, so the various manner of things delivered in Holy Scriptures makes them applicable to our understandings: and what in one kind of delivery seems harsh or obscure in another kind is acceptable, and more easily apprehended. That, which is easy to you, is hard perhaps to me; and what may be thought an impropriety to some great judgments doth many times most properly insinuate the speaker's meaning unto them of meaner capacities.

* * * *

"If it be but to awaken our dulness, and take away our wearisomeness in holy duties, variety is needful. For flesh and blood, as we find by daily experience, loaths those things, wherewithall they are naturally best pleased, if they be too frequent: how much more tedious then will those things be unto us, which are perpetually iterated in the same words, being naturally unpleasing to a carnal ear? Since God in mercy hath provided and permitted, as means to assist our weaknesses, let not such as are strong enough to be without them, condemn the use of such helps in those who, being not so able, must have their affections weaned by degrees from their childish inclinations.

"We see the flesh and the Devil, having for their service thousands of vain songs and profane ballads, stored up in the stationer's warehouses, have nevertheless many Muses perpetually employed for the composing of new strains; and that many hundred pounds are yearly consumed upon them, to the enriching of those merchants; to the shame of our profession; to the corruption of youth; and to the building up of the kingdom of sin and Satan; as it is well known and observed by many of good note in this Reverend Assembly. Yet there having been, for divers ages together, but so many Hymns composed and published, as make in some impressions not above two sheets and a half of paper, for the reverence and practice of devotion unto the honour of God, they are censured impertinent; maliciously exclaimed on; violently opposed; and the author of them seeking, for the needful hire of his labour, but his due, and what strangers should have been suffered to make thereof, is publicly accused, as a man covetously hunting after the world, and an injurious oppressor of the Commonwealth.

* * * *

"My weak fortunes, my troubles, and the chargeableness of a study, that brings with it no outward supply, put me into a kind of necessity to cast my thoughts aside unto worldly respects; but I have since been sorry for it upon better consideration. And as a just reward for my too earnest looking after vain hopes, I do now accept of my present trouble that outwardly is like to impoverish me. And the time thereof draws me the more heedfully to consider it, being just about that season wherein I expected to reap some contentment in the fruition of my labour and expenses. God grant this experience may enrich me another way, and settle my hopes upon more certain things; and that those who accuse me of this imperfection, may examine their own hearts, and if they find them guilty of the like infirmity, learn by mine example to confess their error; and my prayer shall be, that we both may more directly seek God's glory in our undertakings.

"But why should I be the man more accused than all others, for seeking after the just hire of my labours? Am I the only one guilty of studying mine own profit, in the course of my painful endeavours for religious end? I would to God I were; and that no man living save I, were so wicked as to make his own glory and enriching the end and scope of his Christian diligence! For doubtless such an universal piety would be a powerful means of drawing me to repentance. But I believe there be so few that can, with the Apostle clear himself herein, that if none might be permitted to throw at me the stone of reproof, but only they who are free from this weakness, I may walk from St. Michael's Mount in Cornwall to

Dover, and from thence even through our Metropolitan Churches, to the farthest Northern Isles without touch of exception.

"And whereas they object I have compassed a privilege to the public grievance; your Reverences shall perceive how innocent I am from giving cause of such an imputation, if you please to consider the circumstances of his Majesty's grant, with his pious intention, and my carriage in the procuring and execution of it: for I did not, as some of the Stationers have done in the name of many, and by pretending the relief of the poor, whom they may be proved thereby to oppress, monopolize the principal books of sale within this realm, even those wherein the commonwealth have a just interest. which is really one of those monopolies which our State abhors: but having composed a new Book which no man could claim a share in, while it remain mine own, and in mine own power to make public or no; and proposing the same to his Majesty briefly and plainly, without pretence of any bye-respect, I obtained a free and gracious grant to make such benefit thereof as usually heretofore, in like cases his Majesty hath vouchsafed unto others; yea, such as the Stationers would have made of it without a privilege, if so be I had left it in their power.

* * * *

"How unfortunate am I as some think, that having performed a good work do nevertheless hear it exclaimed upon as a frivolous labour; and stand accused for oppressing the people, because a few *Hymns*, containing the praises of God are commanded to be divulged the most convenient way, while such abuses as these aforementioned, and many of an higher nature, may be winked at in my accusers. Yet I say rather, how happy am I, and how much bound to praise God's mercy, who covers the multitude of my transgressions, and still brings me into public question for such actions only as shall upon trial become mine honour; and to the shame of my traducers. For I am confident that I shall in due time be delivered from that, and from all other scandalous imputations, which the world have laid to my charge. And, therefore, whether it be now or hereafter. I am indifferent, and place such assurance in God's word, that I can stay his leisure.

"I procured the King's grant, being the possibility of a temporal blessing, by moving for it where I ought; and as I ought to seek the same, without any man's furtherance: and if it be not in every particular just and convenient that I should enjoy the same, it shall go; and I will venture an utter undoing, rather than make use of any man's friendship to detain it. For God, who hath hitherto provided for me in such a manner, as best befitted both my temporal and spiritual condition, will, I know, continue his provident care of me, while I can have grace to be thankful, and retain the resolution to do my lawful endeavour. Howsoever, let the world conceit of me as it pleaseth, I scorn to enjoy my life, much more any privilege, to the common prejudice: and am able to demonstrate, as shall hereafter appear, that my Book, and the King's Grant, have been maliciously traduced without cause.

* * * *

"I will omit to particularize those many discourtesies which I am offered, and proceed to answer such other objections as they and their abettors have framed, to bring both my *Hymns* and me into contempt.

"And first, they object, forsooth, that they are not worthy to be annexed with their Psalms in metre, in respect of that insufficiency which they have discovered in my expressions. For so harsh and improper do my lines appear to these judicious censurers and their chaplains, that some compare them to *Dod, the Silkman's* late ridiculous translation of the Psalms; which was by authority worthily condemned to the fire. Some term them in scorn, WITHER'S SONNETS; and some, among them, the better to express what opinion they have of their pious use, are pleased to promise that they will procure the *loving ballad-singer with one leg, to sing and sell them about the city;* which base speeches, proceeding from those scoffing Ismaelites, I could well enough brook in respect of mine own person or merit; for their is so much evil, even in the best of my actions, that contempt is the fairest reward which they can justly challenge. Yet when I call to mind with what Christian intentions I was employed upon those Hymns; and how many hours at midnight I spent about them, whilst, it may be, my traducers were either sleeping out their time, or worse employed: when I consider also how many learned and religious men have approved them, and how much their pious use might further the reverence and practice of devotion to the praise of God; it grieves me that there should be in this nation any so

INTRODUCTION. xxiii

wicked as to oppose so Christian a work to so frivolous an end. But when I remember by whom and by what authority that book was allowed and commanded to be made public; and withal, what mystery of iniquity it is that hath conspired against the same, methinks it is an injury not to be tolerated.

"Is it reason, they, who live by books, should be permitted to abuse the authors of their livelihood? Or is it seemly, that those, who, as I said before, are but the pedlars of books, should become their censurers; and, by consequent, both the censurers and depravers of that authority which allowed them? If this be tolerated, the fairest draughts of Apelles shall be daily subject to the foolish criticisms of those arrogant cobblers; and the State shall not be able, ere long to publish any thing but what they have a fancy to approve. For to this pass it is already come, that whatsoever the State dislikes, shall be imprinted and divulged by them, though both absurd and scandalous, with twice more seriousness, than any book lawfully commanded: but let it tend to schism, and they will disperse more underhand in one week, than the Royal Authority shall be able to divulge in a year, toward the settling of unity in the Church.

"I know not what it is which should make my *Book of Hymns* appear so ridiculous unto them, or so unworthy to be annexed to the English Psalm Book, as they pretend. In respect of the matter, it cannot justly be excepted against; for a great part thereof is Canonical Scripture; and the rest also is both agreeable thereunto in every particular, and consonant to the most approved discipline of the Church of England. So that, how squeamishly soever some of their stomachs brook it, they, being allowed by authority, are as fit, I trust, to keep company with David's Psalms, as ROBERT WISDOME's *Turk and Pope*, and those other apocryphal Songs and Prayers, which the Stationers add to the Psalm-Book for their more advantage. Sure I am, that if their additions shall be allowed of by the most voices, yet mine shall be approved of, before those, by the best judgments.

* * * *

"I did not leap of a sudden, and irreverently into this employment; but having consumed almost the years of an apprenticeship in studies of this kind, I entered thereunto conscionably, and in the fear of God; nor have I proceeded without his assistance, as the difficulties and discouragements which I have passed through do witness unto me. For if it be well weighed, how full of short sentences and sudden breakings off, those Scriptures are; how frequently these particles, *for*, *but*, and such like, which are graceful in the original text, will seem to obscure the dependency of sense in the English phrase, if the power of their signification be not heedfully observed in those places: how harsh the music will be, if the chief pauses be not carefully reduced into the same place in the line throughout the whole Hymn, which they have in the first stanza; how many differences must be observed between Lyric Verse, and that which is composed for reading only: how the Translator is tied not to make choice of those fashion stanzas, which are easiest to express the matter in, but to keep that with which he first began: how he is bound, not only to the sense, (according to the liberty used in other translations) but to the very words, or words of the same power with those used in our allowed interpretations: lastly, how precise he must be, when he is forced to express any sentence by circumlocution, to labour still to retain a relish of the holy phrase in his expressions: I say, if all these circumstances be well considered (and how difficult they make it to close up every stanza with a period, or some such point that the voice may decently pause there), I am persuaded a work of this nature, could not have been persisted in, to this conclusion, by a man having so many weaknesses and discouragements as I have had; unless the Almighty had been with me. Nor can I believe that the Devil would have raised up so many maliciously to oppose the same, if it had not tended to God's honour.

" But sure no man will grudge the annexing of the *Book of Hymns* to our metrical Psalms now used, in regard of any faultiness in their expression, if they consider the meanness of that translation. For though some, of no mean degree, are very violent for the maintenance and continuance of their old version, pleading, as the papists do, for many of their trumperies, a long prescription instead of better arguments: yet I know it to be, so much to blame, that no man of understanding can sing many of those Psalms, but with trouble to his devotion. And I dare undertake to demonstrate, that they are not only full of absurdities, solecisms, improprieties, nonsense, and impertinent circumlocutions, to more than twice the length of their originals in some places, but that there are in them many expressions also, quite beside, if not quite contrary, to the meaning of the text; which I would not thus openly have declared, but that even school-boys perceive it; though some, that would be thought wiser, do ignorantly or wilfully protest against an alteration of our singing Psalms. Excuse me, I beseech you, if I seem a little too plain in discovering the faultiness of that, whereof so many are overweening; for I do it not to disparage the pious endeavours of those who took pains in that translation; but rather, commending their laborious and Christian intention, do acknowledge, that, considering the times they lived in, and of what quality they were, they made so worthy an attempt, as may justly shame us, who came after, to see it no better seconded during all the flourishing times which have followed their troublesome age: especially, seeing how curiously our language and expressions are refined in our trivial discourses.

"This hath given the Papist, the Atheist, and the Libertine occasion to scoff at our Christian exercises; and troubles the devotion of many a religious man, who being desirous to sing with his understanding in the congregations, doth often, before he is aware, lose the sense of the Prophet: yea, and sometimes fall upon direct nonsense, among those many impertinent circumlocutions and independencies, which he is for rhyme's sake compelled to wander through in that translation.

"Nevertheless, some I know will be obstinate in defence of their old metre; and I shall seem to them, as one that had presumptuously laid an imputation upon our Church, and unreverently taxed what her authority had commanded; which, I thank God, I am not guilty of. For I well enough know, and your Reverences can witness it, that those metrical Psalms were never commanded to be used in divine service, or in our public congregations, by any canon or ecclesiastical constitution, though many of the vulgar be of that opinion. But whatsoever the Stationers do in their title page pretend to that purpose, they being first allowed for private devotion only, crept into public use by toleration rather than command. Yea, custom hath been hitherto their chief authority; and therefore we may not only lay open their defects to a good purpose, without just blame to ourselves or scandal to the Church, but I hope, charge them also without offence, when a better translation shall come to light. For the mean time there shall be no reason, I am sure, why those should condemn my expressions, while they approve those measures we have hitherto made use of in our devotions.

"But lest the work should be able to justify itself, in spite of their detraction, my adversaries do pick personal quarrels also; alleging that I have undecently intruded upon the divine calling; and that my performances, being but the fruits of a private spirit, are therefore void and unwarrantable. Yea, if we may believe the Stationers, many zealous ministers have taxed me for meddling with a work of that nature, affirming that it was a task fitter for a divine than for me: and so bitterly have many of them as I hear censured me for it in their private conferences, that I have good 'cause to suspect it was rather envy than any thing else which induced most of them to be of that opinion. If it be a work so proper to a divine that no man else ought to have meddled with it, I would some of them had taken it in hand, who give me so little thanks for my labour, that we might have seen with what spirit they are guided. I wonder what divine calling HOPKINS and STERNHOLD had more than I have, that their *metrical Psalms* may be allowed of rather than *my Hymns*. Surely if to have been Groom of the Privy Chamber were sufficient to qualify them, that profession which I am of, * may as well fit me for what I have undertaken, who having first laid the foundation of my studies in one of our famous Universities,† have ever since builded thereon, towards the erecting of such fabrics, as I have now in hand.

"But I would gladly know by what rule those men discern of spirits who condemn my endeavour as the work of a private spirit. The time was, men did judge the tree by his fruit; but now they will judge the fruit by the tree. If I have expressed anything repugnant to the analogy of the Christian faith; or irreverently opposed the orderly and allowed discipline; or dissented in any point from that spirit of verity, which breathes through the Holy Catholic Church, then let that which I have done, be taxed for the work of a private spirit. Or if it may appear that I have undecently intruded myself to intermeddle with those mysteries of our Christian Sanctuary, which the God of order hath by his divine law reserved for those who have according to his ordinance, a

* The Law. † Oxford.

special calling thereunto, then indeed let me be taxed as deserving both punishment and reproof.

"But if, making conscience of my actions, I observed that seemly distance, which may make it appear I intended not upon ought appropriated to the outward ministry; if, like an honest hearted Gibeonite, I have but a little extraordinarily laboured to hew wood and draw water, for the spiritual sacrifices; if according to the art of the Apothecary, I have composed a sweet perfume to offer up to God, in such manner as is proper to my own faculty only; and then brought it to those unto whom the consecration thereof belongs; if keeping my own place, I have laboured for the building up of God's House, as I am bound to do, in offering up of that which God hath given me, and making use with modesty of those gifts which were bestowed on me to that purpose; if, I say, the case be so, what blame-worthy have I done? Why should those disciples, which follow Christ in a nearer place, forbid us from doing good in his name, who follow him further off? Why should they with Joshua forbid Eldad and Medad from prophesying, seeing every good Christian wished with Moses, that all God's people were prophets, and that he would give his spirit to them all?

*　　　*　　　*　　　*

"Let it not therefore, I beseech you, be an imputation unto me, that I have performed a better work than my calling seems to oblige me unto. For though some have taxed me for meddling with that which seems more properly to belong to their profession; it is odds but they are otherwhile as busy in some employments, which would better have beseemed a man of my quality, than a man of my coat; and therefore let us excuse and forgive one another. That which I have done, when it was my own, was subject to any man's censure; but now Authority hath consecrated it, and delivered the same forth for public use, it is no more mine, but the work of Authority which they traduce.

"Let all my writings, privately or publicly dispersed, be examined, from the first Epigram that ever I composed, until the publishing of these Hymns, now traduced by my adversaries; and if there can be found one line savouring of such a mind as may give cause to suspect I undertook that task without that true Christian aim which I ought to have had; or if the performance itself shall make it appear that I proceeded without due preparation; or if you can have any probable testimony that through the course of my life, or by any one scandalous act, I have given that cause of offence, as may disparage my studies, or trouble their devotions to whose use my Hymns are tendered, let those things be laid to my charge, until I find means to disprove and wash away imputations. Sure I am, no man can attempt such a work, with a heart more desirous to be rectified, or more fearful to offend by a negligent performance; and therefore if I wanted an outward calling thereunto, which this reverend Assembly may supply, yet I hope I had that inward calling, which is beyond the power of any to confer."

The anxiety Wither displays in this extract from the Scholar's Purgatory, respecting his Hymns and Songs of the Church, may well be

INTRODUCTION. xxxi

pardoned, for beside his hope of relief from previous necessities by the sale of the work, he had been induced by the favour of the King "to engage his credit almost £300 further to divulge the book," and by the animosity of the Stationers he felt himself deprived even of the means of subsistence. The special pleadings of the poet, however, were of no avail. Self-interest made the Worshipful Company of Stationers inexorable, and the patent granted by King James was to him a dead letter.

But notwithstanding the exertions of the Stationers to keep the Hymns and Songs of the Church "out of print," they will be read and admired so long as the English language is extant. "His language," says Mr. Wilmott, "is unadorned and homely, and the thoughts such as would naturally arise to a calm and benevolent mind. Yet his humblest strains frequently awake a cheerfulness and serenity in the heart of the reader. The spirit of his supplication is so pure and beautiful, that we do not doubt for an instant that the golden sceptre of mercy will be extended to it."

The Hymns and Songs were set to music by Orlando Gibbons, a distinguished musician of the day, and it is thought that a reprint of these old and rare tunes would render the work more acceptable to the public. These tunes are described by Sir John Hawkins as melodies in two parts and excellent in their kind; in them may be traced the germs of several of the most popular church tunes now used in Divine Worship.

In 1625 Wither was a spectator of the great plague which desolated London. This plague broke out in the house of a Frenchman "without the bishop-gate," and the poet has given a glowing description of its ravages, and the effects which it had on society in general, in a poem which he published soon after entitled "Britain's Remembrancer." Wither seems to have lived on the banks of the Thames at the time the plague broke out, and while the rich fled from the devoted city he remained to aid the perishing multitude. He is decidedly an advocate of non-contagion, for he records as a fact that but few sextons and surgeons died of the plague, and that he did not hear of a single death among the market people, who brought provisions into the city. But what is more remarkable, he adds, that in the parish where he resided and where about five hundred died of the plague weekly, not one of the common-bearers of the pestilential corpses fell a victim to its ravages. There is not a more graphic picture of Death and Desolation extant than Britain's Remembrancer gives of this terrible Scourge; and the man who could quietly remain in the midst of it to aid the sick and dying deserves immortal honour for his philanthropy. As Mr. Wilmott justly observes, "It is impossible to contemplate the conduct of Wither during this season of grief without a feeling of admiration and respect." But the Christian poet placed his trust in the protecting care of the Almighty and was safe.

From the date of the plague no mention is made of Wither till the year 1631, when we are told that he assisted the Rev. William Bedwell in the publication of the Tournament of Tottenham. In the following year he published the

INTRODUCTION. xxxiii

"Psalms of David translated into Lyric verse, according to the scope of the Original." He was again favoured with the King's Patent "that this translation should be printed and bound to all Bibles that were sold," but his old enemies the Stationers by their influence set it aside. In Wither's own estimation this version of the Psalms was the best jewel he possessed : and it is certain that it was the best which had yet been written for devotional purposes. Even that harsh critic Johnson awarded him the praise of having done best what he dogmatically asserted "no one could do well."

Wither was in the Netherlands when he published his Psalter. He does not appear to have sojourned long in that country, but the publication of his Emblems, in 1634 seems to have been promoted by his residence there. In his Emblems the poet shewed himself to be a warm supporter of Monarchy and the Church. In various parts he inveighs bitterly against the Puritan spirit of the age. Within a few years, however, after the publication of his Emblems, a great change took place in his sentiments. In the year 1646 he had become, indeed, as fiery a puritan as any in England. The Church was denounced by him as the cause of all the misery in the country: 'her avarice and pride" he asserted had first divided the island; and it was from her the
firebrands came,
That set this empire in a flame.
Alas, how weak a thing is human nature! This change in the sentiments of Wither is evidently the fruit of disappointment. While hope of patronage warmed his breast he firmly supported

the existing institutions of his country, but when poverty stared him in the face as it did at this period; when "death and wasting time" had removed from him those friends from whom to ask a favour was to receive, the poet lost heart, and not only used the pen but unsheathed the sword against the cause he had so long and nobly supported.

Before, however, this change came over the poet, he rendered considerable service to the cause of devotional literature by the publication in 1641 of the Halleluiah, or Britain's Second Remembrancer. This book is very rare, but copious extracts have been given from it by Wither himself in the Fragmenta Prophetica; by Sir Egerton Brydges, in the Censura Literaria; and by Dalrymple, in his selections from the Juvenilia. The touching pathos of many of these hymns have rarely been equalled, and the republication of them would be a boon to the age in which we live. Witness the beautiful Hymn for Anniversary Marriage days:—

> Lord, living here are we
> As fast united yet,
> As when our hands and hearts by thee
> Together first were knit.
> And in a thankful song,
> Now sing we will thy praise,
> For that thou dost as well prolong
> Our loving as our days.
>
> The frowardness that springs
> From our corrupted kind,
> Or from those troublous outward things
> Which may distract the mind;
> Permit not thou, O Lord,
> Our constant love to shake,
> Or to disturb our true accord,
> Or make our hearts to ache

Who would have imagined that the mind from which such tender thoughts as these emanated, could have mingled in the strife and bitterness of party spirit, which was every day and hour becoming stronger and stronger at this period of English History? yet so it was. With the Halleluiah the poetical life of Wither seems to have terminated. He became actively engaged in the earlier part of the civil war; and the "sweetness of his Shepherd's pipe was lost to him for ever." In an address to his Muse written years before this period he writes:—

> Therefore Muse to thee I call,
> Thou (since nothing else avails me)
> Must redeem me from my thrall.
> If thy sweet enchantments fail me,
> Then adieu, life, love, and all.

The latter years of the life of Wither were worn out in strife, in petulant complaints, in penury, and in sorrow. Over this dreary period of the poet's history we draw a veil. The discordant din of politics, war, and fanaticism was to him like as the evil spirit was to Saul: it drove far from him that fine spirit of poesy, which had so long been to him the comfort and solace of his heart. He continued it is true from time to time to pour out rhymes, and that with considerable facility, but the spirit and the life of poetry were no longer discernible in his verse. In a word, the after poetry of Wither chiefly consists of narrations and invectives relative to the strife of Royalists and Parliamentarians.

Wither reaped the bitterest fruits of his tergiversation at the Restoration of the Royal Family. His property was confiscated; and all his MSS.

and books were seized under a warrant from Secretary Nicholas, while he himself was sent to Newgate. He was subsequently removed to the Tower, where he appears to have remained for more than a year. Campbell says that he died in the Tower; but this is a mistake, for he was released on the 27th of July, 1663, after having given bond for his good behaviour.

Before his incarceration in the Tower, Wither appears to have been living in retirement in Hampshire. It is probable he returned thither, but if so he shortly after took up his abode in London. He was living there at the time of the second plague and the great fire of London, as we gather from his Meditations upon the Lord's Prayer, and his Fragmenta Prophetica. In the former he remarks: "During the great mortality yet continuing, and wherein God evidently visited his own household, my little family, consisting of three persons only, was visited and with my dear consort, long engaged in daily expectation of God's diviner purpose concerning our persons; yet with confidence, whether we were smitten or spared, lived or died, it would be in mercy; for having nothing to make us in love with the world, we had placed our hopes upon the world to come."

The pestilence and the fire so thinned and separated the poet's friends, that he contemplated retirement "to a solitary habitation in the place of his nativity," but this intention was abandoned n the advice of some of his few remaining friends. But his end was drawing nigh. His "path had gradually been growing rougher and more painful, as he wound deeper into the vale of years," but it is pleasing to observe from some of the last words traced by the poet's pen that, after all the storms and roughnesses of life his faith remained unshaken, and that he awaited his final summons with the calm fortitude of a genuine Christian. He died on the 2nd of May, 1667, and was buried in the church belonging to the Savoy Hospital in the Strand.

According to Aubrey, Wither married Elizabeth Emerson, of South Lambeth, who was a great wit, and could also write verse. How tenderly he was attached to his consort many touching passages in his poetry testify. No mention is made of her death, but it seems probable that she had preceded him to the tomb. His wife had borne him six children, but one only, a daughter survived her parents.

The private character of Wither was one of almost patriarchal simplicity. It was a reflex of his poetry. As a son, a friend, a parent, and a husband, never did character shine more brightly. Austerely simple and unostentatious he loathed the fawning adulation of the age in which he lived. To use his own language,

> When any bow'd to me with congee's trim,
> All I could do was stand and laugh at him;
> Bless me! I thought what will this coxcomb do,
> When I perceived one reaching at my shoe.

In his habits he was very temperate. His chief indulgence was in the luxury of smoking. In Newgate his pipe was a solace to him, and he gratefully acknowledged God's mercy in wrapping up " a blessing in a weed."

As a politician no praise can be given to Wither. Yet though in reference to politics he was like a reed shaken by every wind, he seems on the whole

d

to have preserved his honesty. He was unbending even to Cromwell, and for this he finally lost the Protector's favour. His political sentiments can scarcely be defined, nor are his religious feelings less difficult to portray. In early life he was a strict Episcopalian, and when he joined the ranks of Republicanism he seems to have forsaken the outward forms of Episcopacy rather than its ordinances. He called himself a Catholic Christian; and asserted that he separated "from no church adhering to the foundations of christianity." Of his inherent piety there can be no question. His writings abound with proofs of the sincerity of his religious profession, and though there is in " all of them somewhat savouring of a natural spirit," yet there is also in all, much "that is dictated by a better spirit than his own." Amidst all his misfortunes, his character was marked by dignity and fortitude,—the result of true piety. Even in the midst of the deepest affliction he could sing,—

> But Lord, though in the dark,
> And in contempt thy servant lies;
> On me there falls a spark
> Of loving kindness from thine eyes.

As a poet Wither ranks high among those who were his contemporaries. His secular poetry contains touches of rural simplicity rarely surpassed; and his sacred poetry reminds the reader of the fine chords of the sweet singer of Israel. There is no exuberant fancy displayed in his verse: he deals not with elaborate metaphors nor produces any striking imagery to enchain the senses; but still by the natural grace and melody of his style, by the touching simplicity of his language, and by the skilful handling of his metre, he carries conviction to the mind of the reader that his verse everywhere contains the fine gold of poetry. Simplicity is a primary quality of genius and never did writer display this quality in richer profusion than the poet Wither. A flower is not the less beautiful for being simple; on the contrary, the rose and the lily vie in beauty with the most gorgeous flowers produced by nature or by art. Just so it is with the language of Wither's poetry compared with that of many of his contemporaries. Faithful to nature and truth he despised their glittering eccentricities, their fantastic images, their inflated diction, their quaint conceits, their forced pathos, and their far-fetched learning; and the result is, that while their verse fails to affect the heart, *his* comes home to every bosom. Nature answers to nature, as in the glass face answers to face; thus demonstrating the high qualities of his poetical genius.

These remarks on the poetical talent of Wither will be borne out by a perusal of his Hymns and Songs; and we intend laying before our readers other works from his pen which will equally testify to his merits as a poet.

EDWARD FARR.

Iver,
July 1st, 1856.

THE HYMNES AND SONGS OF THE CHURCH.

Divided in two Parts.

The first Part comprehends the Canonicall Hymnes, and such parcels of Holy Scripture as may properly be Sung: with some other ancient Songs and Creeds.

The second Part consists of Spirituall Songs, appropriated to the severall Times and Occasions, observable in the Church of England.

Translated and Composed

BY

G. W.

LONDON :
Printed by the Assignes of GEORGE WITHER. 1 6 2 3.
Cum Priuilegio Regis Regali.

TO THE HIGH AND MIGHTY PRINCE,

JAMES,

BY THE GRACE OF GOD, KING OF GREAT BRITAIN,

FRANCE, AND IRELAND, DEFENDER

OF THE FAITH, &C.

MERCY AND PEACE, THROUGH JESUS CHRIST
OUR LORD.

THESE HYMNS, dread Sovereign, having divers ways received life from your Majesty, as well as that approbation which the Church alloweth, are now imprinted according to your royal privilege, to come abroad under your gracious protection. And what I delivered unto your princely view at several times, I here present again, incorporated into one volume. The first part whereof comprehends those canonical Hymns, which were written, and left for our instruction, by the Holy Ghost. And those are not only plainly and briefly expressed in lyric verse, but by their short Prefaces properly applied also to the

Church's particular occasions in these times: insomuch, that, however some neglect them as impertinent, it is thereby apparent, that they appertain no less to us than unto those in whose times they were first composed. And (if the conjecture of many good and learned men deceive them not) the latter part, containing Spiritual Songs, appropriated to the several times and occasions observable in the Church of England (together with brief Arguments, declaring the purpose of those observations) shall become a means both of increasing knowledge, and Christian conformity within your dominions; which, no doubt, your Majesty wisely foresaw, when you pleased to grant and command that these Hymns should be annexed to all Psalm Books in English metre. And I hope you shall thereby increase both the honour of God, and of your Majesty: for these Hymns, and the knowledge which they offer, could no other way, with such certainty, and so little inconvenience, be conveyed to the common people, as by that means which your Majesty hath graciously provided.

And now (maugre their malice, who labour to disparage and suppress these helps to devotion) they shall, I trust, have free scope to work that effect which is desired; and to which end I was encouraged to translate and compose them. For, how meanly soever some men may think of this endeavour, I trust the success shall make it appear,

DEDICATION.

that the Spirit of God was the first mover of the work: wherein, as I have endeavoured to make my expressions such as may not be contemptible to men of best understandings; so I have also laboured to suit them to the nature of the subject, and the common people's capacities, without regard of catching the vain blasts of opinion. The same also hath been the aim of Master Orlando Gibbosn (your Majesty's servant and one of the Gentlemen of your honourable Chapel) in fitting them with tunes: for he hath chosen to make his music agreeable to the matter, and what the common apprehension can best admit, rather than to the curious fancies of the time; which path both of us could more easily have trodden. Not caring, therefore, what any of those shall censure, who are more apt to control than to consider, I commit this to God's blessing, and your favourable protection; humbly beseeching your Majesty to accept of these our endeavours, and praying God to sanctify both us and this work to his glory: wishing, also, most unfeignedly, everlasting consolations to your Majesty, for those temporal comforts you have vouchsafed me, and that felicity here, which may advance your happiness in the life to come. Amen

Your Majesty's
Most loyal Subject,
GEORGE WITHER.

A TABLE OF
THE HYMNS AND SONGS CONTAINED BOTH IN THE FIRST AND SECOND PART OF THIS BOOK.

The first Number declaring the Song, the second the Page.

Hymns found in the Books of Moses, and in the other Books of Holy Scripture, called Hagiographa.

Song	Page
1. The first Song of Moses.	2
2. The Second Song of Moses	6
3. The Song of Deborah, etc.	14
4. The Song of Hannah	23
5. The Lamentation of David	26
6. David's Thanksgiving	29
7. Nehemiah's Prayer	32
8. The Song of Lemuel.	36

The Song of Solomon divided into ten Canticles.

9. The first Canticle	41
10. The Second Canticle	44
11. The third Canticle	47
12. The fourth Canticle	51

CONTENTS.

Song	Page
13. The fifth Canticle	53
14. The sixth Canticle	58
15. The seventh Canticle	61
16. The eighth Canticle	65
17. The ninth Canticle	68
18. The tenth Canticle	73

The Hymns found in the books of the Prophets, with the Lamentations of Jeremiah.

19. The first Song of Esai	77
20. The second Song of Esai	80
21. The third Song of Esai	82
22. The Prayer of Hezekiah	88
23. Hezekiah's Thanksgiving	90
24. The first Lamentation of Jeremiah	94
25. The second Lamentation	102
26. The third Lamentation	109
27. The Fourth Lamentation	117
28. The fifth Lamentation	122
29. The Prayer of Daniel	125
30. The Prayer of Jonah	130
31. The Prayer of Habakuk	133

The Hymns of the New Testament.

32. The Song of our Lady, or Magnificat	140
33. The Song of Zachary, or Benedictus	142
34. The Song of Angels	144
35. The Song of Simeon	146
36. The Song of the Lamb	147

The rest that make up the first part are these.

37. The Ten Commandments	149
38. The Lord's Prayer	152
39. The Apostle's Creed	153

CONTENTS.   xlix

Song	Page
40. A Funeral Song	155
41. The Song of the Three Children	157
42. The Song of St. Ambrose	160
43. The Creed of Athanasius	163
44. Come, Holy Ghost, or Veni Creator	168

THE SECOND PART OF THE HYMNS
AND SONGS OF THE CHURCH.

Spiritual Songs, appropriated to those times, in which are commemorated the principal Mysteries of Christian Religion.

45. The Song for Advent	175
46. For Christmas	178
47. Another for Christmas	179
48. For the Circumcision	181
49 For Twelfth Day	184
50. For the Purification	186
51. The First Day of Lent	189
52. The Annunciation	191
53. Palm Sunday	193
54. Thursday before Easter	195
55. Good Friday	198
56. Easter Day	203
57. Ascension Day	206
58. Whit Sunday	208
59. Trinity Sunday	212
60. Sunday	216

Spiritual Songs appropriated to the Saints Days, most observable throughout the year.

61. For St. Andrew's Day	218
62. For St. Thomas's Day	220

CONTENTS.

Song		Page
63.	St. Stephen's Day.	222
64.	St. John the Evangelist.	224
65.	Innocents' Day.	226
66.	The Conversion of St. Paul	228
67.	St. Matthia's Day.	230
68.	St. Mark's Day.	231
69.	St. Philip and Jacob's Day	233
70.	St. Barnabas's Day	235
71.	St. John the Baptists's Day	237
72.	St. Peter's Day	240
73.	St. James's Day	242
74.	St. Bartholomew's Day.	244
75.	St. Matthew's Day	246
76.	St. Michael's Day.	249
77.	St. Luke's Day.	251
78.	St. Simon and Jude's Day.	253
79.	All Saint's Day.	255

Spiritual Songs fitted for other Solemnities, and to praise God for public Benefits.

80.	For Rogation Week	261
81.	St. George's Day	266
82.	For Public Deliverances	268
83.	For the Communion	271
84.	For Ember Weeks	282
85.	For seasonable Weather	285
86.	For Plenty	287
87.	For Peace	289
88.	For Victory.	291
89.	For Deliverance from Public Sickness	293
90.	For the King	295
	The Author's Hymn	298
	To the Reader	304
	The Tunes	305

THE FIRST PART OF THE

HYMNS AND SONGS OF THE CHURCH.

CONTAINING THOSE WHICH ARE TRANSLATED OUT

OF THE CANONICAL SCRIPTURE,

TOGETHER WITH SUCH OTHER HYMNS AND CREEDS,

AS HAVE ANCIENTLY BEEN SUNG IN

THE CHURCH OF ENGLAND.

THE PREFACE.

PLAINLY false is their supposition, who conceive that the Hymns, Songs, and Elegies of the Old Testament are impertinent to these latter ages of the Church; for, neither the actions nor writings of the ancient Israelites, which are recorded by the Holy Spirit, were permitted to be done or written for their own sakes, so much as that they might be profitable to warn and instruct us of the latter times, according to St. Paul, 1 Cor. x. And, indeed, so much is not only testified by that

Apostle, in the place afore recited, and throughout the Epistle to the Hebrews, but the very names of those Persons and Places, mentioned in these Hymns and Songs, do manifest it, and far better express the nature of that which they mystically point out, than of what they are literally applied unto; as those who will look into their proper significations shall apparently discover. That, therefore, these parcels of Holy Scripture (which are for the most part metre in their original tongue) may be the better remembered, to the glory of God; and the oftener repeated, to those ends for which they were written; they are here disposed into lyric verse, and do make the First Part of this BOOK; which BOOK is called *The Hymns and Songs of the Church;* not for that I would have it thought part of the Church's Liturgy, but because they are made in the person of all the faithful, and do (for the most part) treat of those things which concern the whole Catholic Church.

THE FIRST SONG OF MOSES.

Exod. xv.

THIS Song was composed and sung to praise the Lord for the Israelites' miraculous passage through the Red Sea, and for their delivery from those Egyptians who were there drowned. It may (and should also) be sung in the Christian congregations, or by their particular members, both with respect to the historical and mystical senses thereof: Historically, in commemoration of that particular deliverance, which God had so long ago and so wondrously vouchsafed to his persecuted and afflicted church: Mystically, in acknowledgement of our own powerful deliverance from the bondage of those spiritual adversaries, whereof those were the types: for Pharaoh (signifying *Vengeance*) typified our great enemy, who, with his host of temptations, afflictions, &c., pursueth us in our passage to the spiritual Canaan. The

Red Sea represented our baptism, 1 Cor. x. 2.
By the Dukes and Princes of Edom (mentioned
in this Song) are prefigured those Powers and
Friends of the kingdom of darkness, which are,
or shall be, molested at the news of our regeneration: and therefore this Hymn may very properly be used after the administration of baptism.

THE FIRST SONG.

1.

NOW shall the praises of the Lord be sung;
    For he a most renowned Triumph won:
Both horse and man into the sea he flung;
And them together there hath overthrown.
The Lord is he whose strength doth make me
    strong,
And he is my salvation and my song;
My God, for whom I will a house prepare,
My father's God, whose praise I will declare.

2.

Well knows the Lord to war what doth pertain,
The Lord Almighty is his glorious name:
He Pharaoh's chariots, and his armed train,
Amid the sea, o'erwhelming, overcame:
Those of his army that were most renown'd,
He hath together in the Red Sea drown'd

The deeps a covering over them were thrown,
And to the bottom sunk they like a stone.

3.

Lord, by thy power thy right hand famous grows ;
Thy right hand, Lord, thy foe destroyed hath ;
Thy glory thy opposers overthrows,
And stubble-like consumes them in thy wrath.
A blast but from thy nostrils forth did go,
And up together did the waters flow :
Yea, rolled up on heaps, the liquid flood
Amid the sea, as if congealed, stood.]

4.

I will pursue them (their pursuer cried),
I will o'ertake them, and the spoil enjoy
My lust upon them shall be satisfied :
With sword unsheath'd my hand shall them destroy
Then from thy breath a gale of wind was sent ;
The billows of the sea quite o'er them went ;
And they the mighty waters sunk into,
E'en as a weighty piece of lead will do.

Lord, who like thee among the Gods is there !
In holiness so glorious who may be !
Whose praises so exceeding dreadful are !
In doing wonders, who can equal thee !

Thy glorious right hand thou on high didst rear,
And in the earth they quickly swallowed were.
But thou in mercy onward hast conveyed
Thy people, whose redemption thou hast paid.

6.

Them by thy strength thou hast been pleas'd to bear
Unto a holy dwelling-place of thine:
The nations at report thereof shall fear,
And grieve shall they that dwell in Palestine.
On Edom's princes shall amazement fall;
The mighty men of Moab tremble shall;
And such as in the land of Canaan dwell,
Shall pine away, of this when they hear tell.

7.

They shall be seized with a horrid fear.
Stone-quiet thy right hand shall make them be,
Till passed over, Lord, thy people are;
Till those pass over, that were bought by thee.
For thou shalt make them to thy hill repair,
And plant them there (O Lord) where thou art heir;
E'en there, where thou thy dwelling hast prepar'd,
That holy place, which thine own hands have rear'd.

8.

The Lord shall ever and for ever reign,
His sovereignty shall never have an end;

For when as Pharaoh did into the main,
With chariots and with horsemen, down descend,
The Lord did back again the sea recall,
And with those waters overwhelm'd them all.
But through the very inmost of the same
The seed of Israel safe and dry-shod came.

THE SECOND SONG OF MOSES.

DEUT. xxxii.

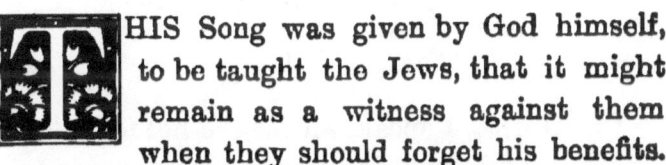HIS Song was given by God himself, to be taught the Jews, that it might remain as a witness against them when they should forget his benefits. For it appears the Divine Wisdom knew that when the Law would be lost or forgotten, a Song might be remembered to posterity. In this Hymn (heaven and earth being called to witness) the Prophet makes first a narration of the Jews' perverseness, and then delivereth prophetically three principal things, wherein divers other particulars are considerable. The first is a prediction of the Jews' idolatry, with the punishments of it. The second is their hatred to Christ, with their *abjection*. And the last is of the calling of the Gentiles. We, therefore, that

have by faith and experience seen the success of what is herein foretold, ought to sing it often, in remembrance of God's Justice and mercy. And (seeing we are all apt enough to become forgetful of our Redeemer's favour as they) we should, by the repetition hereof, seek to stir up our considerations, that (as St. Paul counselleth) we might the better meditate the goodness and severity of God, &c., for if he hath not spared the natural branches, let us take heed, as the same Apostle adviseth, Rom. xi. 24.

SONG II.

Sing this as the First Song.

1.

TO what I speak, an ear, ye heavens, lend,
   And hear, thou earth, what words I utter will;
Like drops of rain my speeches shall descend,
And as the dew my doctrine shall distil,
Like to the smaller rain or tender flowers,
And as upon the grass the greater showers;
For I the Lord's great name will publish now,
That so our God may praised be of you.

2.

He is that Rock, whose works perfection are;
For all his ways with judgment guided be:

OF THE CHURCH.

A God of truth, from all wrong-doing clear,
A truly just and righteous one is he.
Though they themselves defil'd, unlike his sons,
And are a crooked race of froward ones.
Oh mad and foolish nation! why dost thou
Thyself unto the Lord so thankless show?

3.

Thy Father and Redeemer, is not he?
Hath he not made, and now confirm'd thee fast?
Oh call to mind the days that older be,
And weigh the years of many ages past!
For if thy Father, he will tell,
Thy elders also can inform thee well,
How he (the High'st) did Adam's son divide,
And shares for every family did provide.

4.

And how the nation's bounds he did prepare,
In number with the sons of Israel.
For in his people had the Lord his share,
And Jacob for his part allotted fell:
Whom finding in a place possest of none,
(A desert vast, untilled, and unknown)
He taught them there; he led them far and nigh;
And kept them as the apple of his eye.

5.

'Een as an eagle, to provoke her young,
About her nest doth hover here and there,
Spread forth her wings to train her birds along,
And sometimes on her back her younglings bear:
Right so the Lord conducted them alone,
When for his aid strange God with him was none.
Then on the high lands of the earth he set,
Where they the plenties of the field might eat.

6.

For them he made the rock with honey flow,
He drained oil from stones, and them did feed
With milk of sheep, with butter of the cow,
With goats, fat lambs, and rams of Bashan breed.
The finest of the wheat he made their food,
And of the grape they drank the purest blood :
But, herewithal, unthankful Israel
So fat became, he kicked with his heel.

7.

Grown fat, and with their grossness covered o'er,
Their God, their Maker, they did soon forsake :
Their Rock of health regarded was no more,
But with strange Gods him jealous they did make.
To move his wrath they hateful things devis'd ;
To devils in his stead they sacrific'd ;

OF THE CHURCH.

To Gods unknown, that new invented were,
And such as their forefathers did not fear.

8.

They minded not the Rock who them begat,
But quite forgot the God that form'd them hath;
Which when the Lord perceiv'd, it made him hate
His sons and daughters, moving him to wrath.
To mark their end, said he, I'll hide my face,
For they are faithless sons of froward race;
My wrath, with what is not a God, they move,
And my displeasure with their follies prove.

9.

And I, by those that are no people, yet
Their wrathful jealousy will move for this;
And by a foolish nation make them fret;
For in my wrath, a fire inflamed is,
And down to hell the earth consume it shall,
E'en to the mountains' bottoms, fruit and all.
In heaps upon them mischiefs will I throw,
And shoot mine arrows till I have no mo'.*

10.

With hunger parched, and consum'd with heat,
I will enforce them to a bitter end;

* More.

The teeth of beasts upon them will I set,
And will the poisonous dust-fed serpent send.
The sword without, and fear within, shall slay
Maids, young men, babes, and him whose hair is
  gray.
Yea, I had vowed to spread them here, and there ;
Men might forget that such a people were.

11.

But this the foe compell'd me to delay,
Lest that their adversaries (prouder grown)
Should (when they heard it) thus presume to say
This, not the Lord, but our high hand hath done.
For in this people no discretion is ;
Nor can their dulness reach to judge of this.
O had they wisdom this to comprehend,
That so they might bethink them of their end.

12.

How should one make a thousand run away,
Or two men put ten thousand to the foil,*
Except their Rock had sold them for a prey,
And that the Lord had clos'd them up the while;
For though our foes themselves the judges were,
Their God they cannot with our God compare :
But they have vines like those that Sodom yields
And such as are within Gomorrha fields.

* Flight.

13.

They bear the grapes of gall upon their vine ;
Extremely bitter are their clusters all ;
Yea, made of dragon's venom is their wine,
And of the cruel asp's infectious gall.
And can this (ever) be forgot of me ?
Or not be sealed where my treasures be ?
Sure, mine is vengeance ; and I will repay ;
Their feet shall slide at their appointed day.

14.

Their time of ruin near at hand is come ;
Those things that shall befall them haste will make;
For then the Lord shall give his people doom,
And on his servants kind compassion take,
When he perceives their strength bereft and gone,
And that in prison they are left alone.
Where are their gods become ? he that shall say ;
Their rock, on whom affiance they did lay ?

15.

Who ate the fattest of their sacrifice ?
Who of their drink oblations drank the wine ?
Let those unto their succour now arise,
And under their protection them enshrine.
Behold, consider now that I am He,
And that there is no other God with me.

I kill, and make alive; I wound, I cure;
And there is none can from my hand assure.

16.

For up to heav'n on high my hand I rear,
And (as I live for ever) this I say,
When I my shining sword to whet prepare,
And shall my hand to acting vengeance lay,
I will not cease till I my foes requite,
And am avenged on all that bear me spite:
But in their blood, which I shall make to flow,
Will steep mine arrows till they drunken grow.

17.

My sword shall eat the flesh and blood of thoes,
Who shall be either slain or brought in thrall,
When I begin this vengeance on my foes,
Sing therefore with his people, nations all!
For he his servants' blood with blood will pay,
And due avengement on his foes will lay.
But to his land compassion he will show,
And on his people mercy shall bestow.

THE SONG OF DEBORAH AND BARAK.

JUDGES V.

THIS Hymn was composed to glorify God for the great overthrow given to Sisera, who coming armed with many hundred chariots of iron against the poor oppressed Israelites (when they had not a sword or spear among forty thousand of them) was nevertheless miraculously discomfited; to shew the unbelieving people that the Lord only is the God of battles, and that he is both able, and doth often, deliver his Church without the ordinary means. By the repetition hereof we praise God, in commemorating one of the great deliverances heretofore vouchsafed to his Church. And in these times of fear and wavering, we may also, by this memorable example of God's providence, strengthen our faith, which is many times weakened by the outward power, prosperity, or vain boastings of the Church's adversaries, who shall (doubtless) be at last shamefully ruined (according to the prophetical imprecation concluding this Song), notwithstanding their many likelihoods of prevailing. Yea, then, perhaps shall that destruction come on them, to God's greater glory, when our estate seems to be most desperate.

SONG III.

1.

SING praises, Israel to the Lord,
　That thee avenged so,
When to the fight with free accord,
The people forth did go.
　　You Kings, give ear,
　　You Princes, hear,
　While to the Lord I raise,
　　My voice aloud,
　　And sing to God,
　The Lord of Israel praise.

2.

When thou departedst, Lord, from Seir,
When thou left's Edom field,
Earth shook, the heaven's dropped there,
The clouds did water yield.
　　Lord, at thy sight,
　　A trembling fright,
　Upon the mountains fell:
　　E'en at thy look,
　　Mount Sinai shook,
　Lord God of Israel.

OF THE CHURCH. 15

3.

Not long ago, in Shamghar's days,
Old Anath's valiant son;
And late in Jael's time, the ways
Frequented were of none:
  The passengers
  Were wanderers
 In crooked paths unknown;
  And none durst dwell
  Through Israel,
But in a walled town.

4.

Until I, Deborah, arose
(Who rose a mother there)
In Israel, when new Gods they chose,
That fill'd their gates with war;
  And they had there
  Nor shield nor spear
 In their possession then,
  To arm for fight
  One Israelite
'Mong forty thousand men.

5

To those that Israel's Captains are
My heart doth much incline;

To those, I mean, that willing were;
O Lord! the praise be thine.
  Sing ye for this,
  Whose use it is
To ride on asses gray,
  All ye that yet
  In Middin set,
Or travel by the way.

6.

The place where they their waters drew,
From archers now is clear;
The Lord's uprightness they shall shew,
And his just dealing there.
  The hamlets all
  Through Israel shall
His righteousness record;
  And down unto
  The gates shall go
The people of the Lord.

7.

Arise, O Deborah, arise.
Rise, rise, and sing a song;
Abinoam's son, O Barak, rise;
Thy captives haste along;
  Their princes all
  By him made thrall,

To the survivor be,
  To triumph on
  The Mighty One,
The Lord vouchsafed me.

8.

A root from out of Ephraim
'Gainst Amalek arose,
And (of the people) next to him
The Benjamites were those
    From Machir (where
    Good leaders are)
  Came well experienc'd men :
    And they came down,
    From Zabulon,
  That handle well the pen.

9.

Along with Deborah did go
The Lords of Isacha ;
With Isachar, e'en Barak too,
Was one among them there.
    He forth was sent,
    And marching went
  On foot the lower way.
    For Reuben (where
    Divisions were)
  Right thoughtful hearts had they.

10.

The bleating of the flocks to hear,
O wherefore did'st thou stay?
For Reuben (where divisions were)
Right thoughtful hearts had they.
    But why did they
    Of Gilead stay
On Jordan's other side?
    And wherefore then
    Did'st thou, O Dan,
Within thy tents abide?

11.

Among his harbours, lurking by
The sea-side Asher lay;
But Zabulon and Nephthali
Kept not themselves away.
    They people are,
    Who fearless dare
Their lives to death expose;
    And did not yield
    The hilly field,
Though Kings did them oppose.

12.

With them the Canaanitish kings
At Tana'ch fought that day,

OF THE CHURCH.

Close by Megiddo's water-springs,
Yet bore no prize away.
 For, lo! the stars
 Fought in their spheres;
'Gainst Sisera, fought they.
 And some (by force)
 The water-course
Of Kishon swept away.

13.

E'en Kishon river, which was long
A famous torrent known.
Oh, thou, my soul! oh, thou the strong
Hast bravely trodden down.
 Their horse (whose pace
 So lofty was)
Their hoofs with prancing wound;
 Those of the strong.
 That kick'd and flung,
And fiercely beat the ground.

14.

A heavy curse on Meroz lay;
Curst be her dwellers all.
The Angel of the Lord did say,
That city curse you shall.
 And therefore, this
 Accursing is:

They came not to the fight,
    To help the Lord
    (To help the Lord)
Against the men of might.

15.

But, blest be Jael, Heber's spouse,
The Kenite: blest be she,
More than all women are, of those
That use in tents to be.
    To him did she
    Give milk when he
Did water only wish;
    And butter set,
    For him to eat,
Upon a lordly dish.

16.

She in her left hand took a nail,
And rais'd up in the right
A workman's hammer, wherewithal
She Sisera did smite:
    His head she took,
    When she had struck
His pierced temples through:
    He fell withal
    And in the fall
He at her feet did bow.

17.

He at her feet did bow his head,
Fell down, and life forsook.
Meanwhile his longing mother did
From out her window look;
    Thus crying at
    The latticed grate,
' Why stays his chariot so,
    From hasting home?
    Oh! wherefore come
His chariot wheels so slow?'

18.

As thus she spake, her ladies wise
To her an answer gave;
Yea, to herself, herself replies;
' Sure, sped (saith she) they have:
    And all this while
    They part the spoil;
A damsel, one or tway,*
    Each homeward bears,
    And Sisera shares
A party-coloured prey.

19.

Of needle-work, both sides of it
In divers colours are:

---

* Two.

E'en such as doth his neck befit,
That useth spoils to wear.'
   So, Lord, still so
   Thy foes o'erthrow;
But who in thee delight,
   Oh let them be
   Sun-like, when he
Ascendeth in his might.

THE SONG OF HANNAH.

1 Sam. ii. 1.

HANNAH, the wife of Elkanah, being barren (and therefore upbraided and vexed by Peninnah, her husband's other wife), prayed unto the Lord for a Son; and having obtained him, glorified God in this Song, for delivering her from the contempt of her adversary. By Hannah (which signifieth *Grace* or *Gracious*) was the Church of Christ represented: and by Peninnah (signifying *Despised*, or *Forsaken*) was figured the Jewish Synagogue: this Song, therefore, is to be understood as a mystical prophecy of that abjection of the Jews, and calling of the Gentiles, which was fulfilled upon the birth of Jesus Christ, our true Samuel; at whose conception the blessed Virgin Mary, in her *Magnificat*, acknowledged the verifying of many particulars foretold in this Song; even almost in the same words. In memorial, therefore, of these mysteries, we ought to sing this Hymn, to comfort us, also, against the pride and arrogancy of those who, by reason of their multitudes, shall scorn and upbraid the true Church, as mother only of a few and obscure children. And we may use it likewise to praise God for that fruitfulness which he hath given to our Holy Mother, who hath lately had many children advanced to be Kings, and to sit on the most eminent thrones of glory in the earth, according to this prophetical Song.

SONG IV.

1.

NOW in the Lord my heart doth pleasure take;
My horn is in the Lord advanced high:
And to my foes an answer I will make,
Because in his salvation joy'd am I.
Like him there is not any Holy One;
And other Lord beside him there is none.

2.

Nor like our God another God is there:
So proudly vaunt not, then, as heretofore;

But let your tongues from henceforth now forbear
All vain presuming words for evermore.
For why ? the Lord is God, who all things knows
And doth each purpose to his end dispose.

3.

Now broken is their bow that once were stout;
And girt with vigour they that stumbled are.
The full themselves for bread have hired out.
Which now they need not do, that hungry were
The barren womb doth seven children own,
And she that once had many, weak is grown.

4.

The Lord doth slay ; and he revives the slain;
He to the grave doth bring, and back he bears.
The Lord makes poor and rich he makes again!
He throweth down, and up on high he rears.
He from the dust and from the dunghill brings
The beggar and the poor to sit with Kings.

5.

He rears them to inherit glory's throne;
For why? the Lord's the earth's upholders are;
The world hath he erected thereupon ;
He to the footing of his saints hath care;
But dumb in darkness sinners shall remain,
For in their strength shall men be strong in vain.

6.

The Lord will to destruction bring them all,
(E'en every one) that shall with him contend.
From out of heav'n he thunder on them shall,
And judge the world unto the farthest end.
With strength and power his king he will supply,
And raise the horn of his Anointed high.

THE LAMENTATION OF DAVID OVER SAUL AND JONATHAN HIS SON.

2 SAM. i. 17.

IN this funeral Elegy David bewaileth the death of Saul and Jonathan ; from whence these observations may be collected. First, that the slaughter of a valiant Prince is an outward blemish, and just cause of sorrow in the State. Secondly, that the insulting of an adversary is not the least affliction. Thirdly, that the mountains of Gilboa are accursed to this day ; for by Gilboa (which is interpreted *slippery* or *inconstant*) is mystically understood that irresolution or despair, by which men fall into the power of their spiritual adversary. Fourthly, we hence may learn to commemorate those things which are praise-worthy, even in our enemy. Lastly, it sheweth us that wise and good men may tender one friend more affectionately than another; and that if it misbeseems them not to bewail their death. This is to be sung historically for our instruction in the particulars before mentioned; and may be observed as a pattern for our funeral poems.

SONG V.

1.

THY beauty, Israel, is gone;
   Slain in the places high is he;
The mighty now are overthrown;
O thus how cometh it to be!
Let not this news their streets throughout,
In Gath or Askalon, be told;
For fear Philistia's daughters flout,*
Lest vaunt the uncircumcised should.

2.

On you, hereafter, let no dew,
You mountains of Gilboa, fall:
Let there be neither showers on you,
Nor fields that breed an offering shall.

* Rejoice.

For there with shame away was thrown
The target of the strong (alas),
The shield of Saul, e'en as of one,
That ne'er with oil anointed was.

3.

Nor from their blood that slaughter'd lay,
Nor from the fat of strong men slain,
Came Jonathan his bow away,
Nor drew forth Saul his sword in vain.
In lifetime they were lovely fair,
In death they undivided are.
More swift than eagles of the air,
And stronger they than lions were.

4.

Weep Israel's daughters, weep for Saul,
Who you with scarlet hath array'd;
Who clothed you with pleasures all,
And on your garments gold hath laid.
How comes it he, that mighty was,
The foil in battle doth sustain!
Thou, Jonathan, oh thou (alas)
Upon thy places high wert slain!

5.

And much distressed is my heart,
My brother Jonathan, for thee;

My very dear delight thou wert,
And wondrous was thy love to me:
So wondrous, it surpassed far
The love of women (every way).
Oh, how the mighty fallen are!
How warlike instruments decay!

DAVID'S THANKSGIVING.

1 Chron. xxix. 10.

ING David having, by persuasions and his own liberal example, stirred up the people to a bountiful benevolence toward the building of God's House, praised him for that willing and cheerful free-offering. And in this thanksgiving we observe this method: First, he acknowledgeth God's blessedness, Greatness, Power, Glory, Victory, Majesty, Bounty, with the like; and confesseth in general that Honour and Riches, Strength with all other good things, are at the Almighty's disposing. Secondly, he therefore praiseth the Lord, and acknowledgeth also, that his and the people's willingness to give, came not of themselves, but was God's own proper gift (as well as that which they had given. Lastly, he prayeth for the continuance of

God's blessing, both upon their purposes and endeavours; and that their benevolence may be disposed to that end for which it was given. This Song may be very properly used, whensoever among us there hath been any free and liberal contributions to good and pious ends. And to fit the same the better to such purposes, the persons and some few circumstances are a little changed in this translation.

SONG VI.

Sing this as the fifth Song.

1.

OH, Lord, our everlasting God!
    Bliss, Greatness, Power and Praise is thine:
With thee have conquests their abode,
And glorious Majesty divine.
All things that earth and heaven afford,
Thou at thine own disposing hast,
To thee belongs the kingdom, Lord,
And thou for head o'er all art plac'd.

2.

Thou wealth and honour dost command;
To thee made subject all things be:
Both strength and power are in thine hand,
To be dispos'd as pleaseth thee.

And now to thee our God, therefore,
A Song of Thankfulness we frame;
(That what we owe we may restore),
And glorify thy glorious Name.

3.

But what, or who are we (alas)
That we in giving are so free!
Thine own before, our offering was,
And all we have we have from thee.
For we are guests and strangers here,
As were our fathers in thy sight,
Our days but shadow-like appear,
And suddenly they take their flight.

4.

This offering Lord our God, which thus
We for thy namesake have bestown,
Derived was from thee to us;
And that we give is all thine own.
O God! thou prov'st the heart we know,
And dost affect uprightness there;
With gladness, therefore, we bestow
What we have freely offered here.

5.

Still thou (O Lord our God) incline
Their meaning, who the people be;

And ever let the hearts of thine
Be thus prepared unto thee.
Yea, give us perfect hearts, we pray,
That we thy precepts err not from,
And grant, our contribution may
An honour to thy name become!

THE PRAYER OF NEHEMIAH.

Nehem. i. 5.

EHEMIAH, determining (as the story sheweth) to move Artaxerxes for the repairs of the City and the House of the Lord, first made ‚this Prayer, wherein, having acknowledged the Majesty, Justice, and Mercy of God, he confesseth the heinousness of his and his people's sins; desireth forgiveness; entreateth for the people's deliverance from captivity; and requesteth he may find favour in the sight of the King his master. Now we who by regeneration are the sons of Israel (and such as in a spiritual sense, may be said also to be dispersed among the heathen, as often as we are carried captive by the heathenish concupiscences and vanities of the world) even we may, in a literal sense, make use of this excellent form of confession, before our several petitions. And doubtless a faithful using

of these, the Holy Ghost's own words (with remembrance of the happy success they heretofore had) will much strengthen and increase the hope, confidence, and comfort of him that prayeth; who, changing the two last lines only, may appropriate it to any necessity. For example, if it be to be sung before labour, conclude it thus, "and be thou pleased, O Lord, to bless our labours with a good success." If before a journey, thus, "And, Lord, all dangers keep us from,—Both going forth and coming home." If before a battle, thus, "And be thou pleased, in the fight,—To make us victors by thy might." If in the time of famine, thus, "And, Lord, vouchsafe thou, in this need,—Our souls and bodies both to feed." If before a sermon, &c. thus, "And grant that we, Lord, in thy fear,—May to our profit speak and hear." And the like, as occasion requires.

SONG VII.

Sing this as the Ninth Song.

1.

L ORD God of Heav'n! who only art
The Mighty God, and full of fear;
Who never promise-breaker wert,
But ever shewing mercy there,

Where men affection bear to thee,
And of thy laws observers be.

2.

Give ear, and ope thine eyes, I pray,
That heard thy servant's suit may be;
Made in thy presence night and day,
For Israel's seed, that serveth thee,
For Israel's seed, who (I confess)
Against thee grievously transgress.

3.

I and my father's house did sin;
Corrupted all our actions be;
And disrespective we have been
Of statutes, judgments, and decree:
Of these, which to retain so fast,
Thy servant Moses charg'd thou hast.

4.

O yet remember thou, I pray,
These words, which thou didst heretofore
Unto thy servant Moses say.
If e'er (saidst thou) they vex me more,
I will disperse them everywhere,
Among the nations here and there.

5.

But if to me they shall convert,
To do those things my law contain,
Though spread to heav'n's extremest part,
I would collect them thence again,
And bring them there to make repose,
Where I to place my name have chose.

6.

Now these thy people are (of right)
Thy servants who to thee belong,
Whom thou hast purchas'd by thy might,
And by thine arm exceeding strong;
Oh! let thine ear, Lord, I thee pray,
Attentive be to what I say.

7.

The prayer of thy servant hear,
Oh, hear thy servants when they pray,
(Who willing are thy name to fear)
Thy servant prosper thou to day;
And be thou pleas'd to grant that he
May favour'd in thy presence be!

THE SONG OF KING LEMUEL.

Prov. xxxi., 10.

THIS Song is alphabetical in the original. It contains an admirable description of a good wife; and these three things are here principally considered; the advantage her husband receiveth by her; the commendable virtues she hath in herself; and the reward that follows her. Her husband's advantages are these: A quiet heart free from jealousy or distrust of her; a rich estate, without oppressing others; and a place of honour in the commonwealth. Her virtues are industry, providence, cheerfulness, courage, and unweariedness in providing for and disposing of her temporal affairs. Moreover, continual love to her husband; liberality to the poor; government of her tongue; and heedfulness to those courses her household takes. Her reward is this; her husband is confident in her: she shall have comfort of her labours; her posterity shall bless her; her husband shall praise her above other women; she shall be honoured in life, and have joy at her death. It is indeed an excellent Marriage Song, fit to be used at the solemnizing of those rites; for it ministereth instruction becoming that occasion; yea, perhaps the music of it would stir up good affections also (where unpleasing discords are now heard) if it were often sung in private families.

SONG VIII.

Sing this as the sixth Song.

1.

WHO finds a woman good and wise,
    A gem more worth than pearls hath got
Her husbands heart on her relies;
To live by spoil he needeth not.
His comfort all his life is she;
No wrong she willingly will do;
For wool and flax her searches be,
And cheerful hands she puts thereto.

2.

The merchant ship resembling right,
Her food she from afar doth fet,*
Ere day she wakes, that give she might
Her maids their task, her household meat.
A field she views, and that she buys;
Her hand doth plant a vineyard there;
Her loins with courage up she ties,
Her arms with vigour strengthened are.

* Bring.

3.

If in her work she profit feel,
By night her candle goes not out:
She puts her finger to the wheel,
Her hand the spindle twirls about,
To such as poor and needy are
Her hand (yea, both hands) reacheth she.
The winter none of hers doth fear,
For double-cloth'd her household be.

4.

She mantles maketh, wrought by hand,
And silk, and purple clothing gets,
Among the rulers of the land
(Known in the gate) her husband sits.
For sale fine linen weaveth she,
And girdles to the merchant sends.
Renown and strength her clothing be,
And joy her later time attends.

5.

She speaks discreetly when she talks;
The law of grace her tongue hath learn'd;
She heeds the way her household walks,
And feedeth not on bread unearn'd.
Her children rise, and blest her call:
Her husband thus applaudeth her,

Oh, thou hast far surpass'd them all,
Thou many daughters thriving are!

6.

Deceitful favour quickly wears,
And beauty suddenly decays;
But, if the Lord she truly fears,
That woman well deserveth praise,
The fruit her handywork obtains:
Without repining grant her that,
And yield her what her labour gains,
To do her honour in the gate.

THE SONG OF SONGS.

THE PREFACE.

SUCH is the mercy of God, that he taketh advantage even of our natural affections, to beget in our souls an apprehension of his love, and of the mysteries which tend to our true happiness; so fitting his divine expressions to the several inclinations of men, that means might be provided to win some of all. For otherwhile he doth it by comparing the same to the glories of a temporal kingdom, to win such as are most desirous of honours. Sometimes

OF THE CHURCH.

he illustrates it by treasures, gold, and precious stones, &c., the better to allure such as are tempted with things of that nature. And divers other ways also, as appears throughout the book of God. But in this Song of Solomon (wherein is mystically expressed the mutual affection betwixt Christ and his Church, with the chief passages thereof throughout all ages, from Abel to the last judgement, at which time their blessed marraige shall be fully consummated), he doth most movingly impart unto us the ravishing contentments of the divine love, by comparing it to that delight which is conceived in the strongest, the commonest, the most pleasing, the most natural, and the most commendable of our affections. And doubtless it powerfully prevaileth to the enflaming their spiritual love, who seek rightly to understand and apply the mysteries and expressions herein contained. Let no man, therefore, presume to sing, or repeat in a carnal sense, what is here spiritually intended, upon pain of God's heavy indignation. Nor let the wisdom of flesh and blood vainly neglect God's favour, in offering this for the comfort of such as will rightly apply the same; because some atheists and sensual men shall perhaps turn this grace of God into wantonness, to their own condemnation.

THE FIRST CANTICLE.

IN this Canticle is first expressed that longing which the whole Catholic Church had for the embraces of her Redeemer (from the time of Abel till his first coming), with her acknowledgment of his ravishing excellencies; her desire to be drawn after him; and her confession of that joyful happiness which will arise from his favours. Secondly, the particular Church of the Gentiles is brought in entreating an undespised union with the Synagogue of the Jews, both confessing and excusing her blemishes. Thirdly, the whole Catholic Church is again introduced as desiring to be fed and guided by her beloved Shepherd. Fourthly, her petition is most graciously answered, and she directed to follow the steps of the holy Patriarchs and Prophets. Finally, Christ setteth forth the power and rich graces of his Spouse, with what other ornaments he will prepare for her. This Canticle we may sing to the stirring up of our spiritual love; having first seriously meditated these things, to wit, That desire we ought to have in our souls to be joined to Christ; the excellency of his perfections; the backwardness of our human nature to entertain his love; the deformity and damage we sustain, till we be received into the communion of saints; the readiness of Christ to receive and direct us; the pleasure he will take in our love; and the provision he will make for the further beautifying of our souls.

SONG IX.

1.

COME, kiss me with those lips of thine;
    For better are thy loves than wine;
  And as the powered* ointments be,
Such is the savor of thy name.
And for the sweetness of the same,
    The virgins are in love with thee.

2.

Begin but thou to draw me on,
And then we after thee will run;
  Oh, King, thy chambers bring me to;
So we in thee delight shall find,
And more than wine thy love will find,
  And love thee as the righteous do.

3.

And, daughters of Jerusalem,
I pray you do not me contemn,

* Poured forth.

Because that black I now appear;
For I as lovely am (I know)
As Kedar tents (appear in show)
  Or Solomon his curtains are.

4.

Though black I am, regard it not;
It is but sunbeam I have got,
  Whereof my mother's sons were cause;
Their vineyard keeper me they made,
(Through envy which to me they had)
  So my own vine neglected was.

5.

Thou whom my soul doth best affect,
Unto thy pastures me direct,
  Where thou at noon art stretch'd along;
For why should I be straggling spied,
Like her that loves to turn aside,
  Thy fellow shepherd's flocks among?

6.

Oh, fairest of all womankind!
(If him thou know not where to find)
  Go where the paths of cattle are;
Their tracks of footsteps stray not from,
Till to the shepherds' tents thou come,
  And feed thy tender kidlings there.

7.

> My love thou art, of greater force
> Than Pharoah's troops of chariot horse:
>   Thy cheeks and neck made lovely be,
> With rows of stones, and many a chain,
> And we gold borders will ordain,
>   Beset with silver studs for thee.

THE SECOND CANTICLE.

THIS Song seemeth to set forth the mystery of Christ his Incarnation, whereby the Church's first petition (mentioned in the former Canticle) is accomplished. And herein these particulars appear to be mystically expressed:—His birth and repose between the two Testaments, with his sweet and sanctifying operations. Secondly, the Church's acknowledgment of her Redeemer's beauty, innocency, and delightfulness; with how pleasant and incorruptible an habitation is prepared for those lovers; and what excellent privileges she hath by his favour. Thirdly, Christ and his Church do (as two lovers) interchangeably prefer one another before all others, by way of comparison. Fourthly, the spouse's spiritual love-sick passions are expressed. And lastly (she having declared how she is enclosed in his embraces), there is warning given that their sweet union be not disturbed.—This Canticle may properly be sung upon the feast of Christ's Nativity, or at any other time; we having first prepared ourselves by a fruitful meditating the particular mysteries of the Song.

SONG X.

Sing this as the Ninth Song.

1.

WHILE that the King was at repast,
    My Spikenard his perfumings cast;
And twixt my breast repos'd my dear;
My love, who is as sweet to me
As myrrh or camphor bundles be,
    Which at En-gedi vineyards are.

2.

Lo, thou art fair; lo thou, my love!
Art fair, and eyed like the dove!*
    Thou fair and pleasant art, my dear;
And lo, our bed with flowers is strowed,

* Hast eyes like those of the dove.

Our house is beam'd with cedar wood,
And of the fir our rafters are.

3.

I am the Rose that Sharon yields,
The Rose and Lily of the fields,
   And flower of all the dales below ;
My love among the daughters shows,
As when a sweet and beauteous rose
   Amid her bush of thorns doth grow.

4.

Among the sons, such is my dear,
As doth an apple-tree appear,
   Within a shrubby forest plac't ;
I sat me down beneath his shade,
(Whereto a great desire I had)
   And sweet his fruit was to my taste.

5.

Me to his banquet-house he bare,
E'en where his wine provisions are,
   And there his love my banner was ;
With flagons me from fainting stay,
With apples comfort me, I pray,
   For I am sick of love (alas) !

6.

My head with his left hand he stay'd,
His right hand over me he laid ;
  And by the harts and roes (said he)
You, daughters of Jerusalem,
Stir not (for you I charge by them)
  Nor wake my love, till pleas'd she be.

THE THIRD CANTICLE.

BY contemplating this Canticle we may be mystically informed of Christ's calling his Church in the apostles, and of her estate in the beginning of Christianity, when he went from place to place (as a hind over the mountains), to further the work of our redemption, moving his disciples (and in them his Church) to follow him, by shewing his divinity a little and a little (as it were) through the grate and from behind the wall of his *humanity*. Moreover, the spring-like season of the Gospel, after the cloudy and winter-like time under the law, is here set forth. And then the Church, having petitioned that the curtains of the ceremonial law might be so drawn away, as that she may both hear and see her

Beloved in his unveiled perfections; she requesteth also, that the sly enemies of his vineyard may be destroyed. She rejoiceth likewise in their mutual looks; and prayeth him, that while the day of grace lasteth, she may on all occasions enjoy his speedy consolations. Lastly, the Church confesseth how blindly she sought Christ during the night of the law; how diligently (and through what afflictions) she searched after him; how at length she found him; where also, and with what affections, she entertained him; and so concludes, as in the former Canticle. It ought therefore to be sung with reverence, and consideration of the mysteries therein contained.

SONG XI.

Sing this as the Fifth Song.

1.

I HEAR my Love, and him I see
 Come leaping by the mountains there;
Lo, o'er the hillocks trippeth he,
And roe or stag-like doth appear.
Lo, from behind the wall he pries;*
Now at the window-grate is he:
Now speaks my dear, and says, Arise,
My love, my fair, and come with me!

* Looks.

2.

Lo, winter's past, and come the spring,
The rain is gone, the weather's clear;
The season wooes the birds to sing,
And on the earth the flowers appear;
The turtle croweth in our field,
Young figs the fig-tree down doth weigh,
The blossomed vines a savour yield;
Rise, love, my fair, and come away.

3.

My Dove, that art obscured where
The rock's dark stairs do thee infold;
Thy voice (thy sweet voice) let me hear,
And thee (that lovely sight) behold.
Those foxes' cubs, the vines that mar,
Go take us whilst the grapes be young.
My love's am I, and mine's my dear,
Who feeds the lily flowers among.

4.

While break of day, when shades depart,
Return, my well-beloved one,
E'en as a roe or lusty hart,
That doth on Bether mountains run.
For him that to my soul is dear,
Within my bed by night I sought;

I sought, but him I found not there;
Thus therefore with myself I thought:

5.

I'll rise, and round the city wend;*
Through lanes and open ways I'll go,
That I my soul's delight may find.
So there I sought, and missed him too.
The city-watch me lighted on,
Them asked I for my soul's delight;
And, somewhat past them being gone,
My soul's beloved found I straight.

6.

Whom there in my embrace I caught,
And him forsook I not, till he
Into my mother's house I brought,
Her chamber who conceived me.
You daughters of Jerusalem,
Stir not (by field-bred harts and roes,
For you I do adjure by them)
Nor wake my love, till she dispose.

* Walk.

THE FOURTH CANTICLE.

HERE the Royal Prophet first singeth Christ, his going forth to preach the Gospel, metaphorically expressing it (and as it were) by way of admiration, at the excellent name thereof. Next he mentioneth his couch (or resting-place), meaning either the church, or else that bed of his humanity, which the holy fathers and pastors of the church (as her valiant champions), defended by the sword of God's word against infidels, hereticks, and all the powers and terrors of the kingdom of darkness. Then he mystically describeth that palace, throne, or abiding place of Christ, together with the glory of it, as well in regard of the precious matter of each several part, as in respect of the form and beauty of the whole fabrick. And lastly, he exhorteth all the faithful, (under the name of the daughters of Sion) to contemplate seriously the excellent glory of Christ, when (by his incarnation) the Deity was espoused to the humanity. In singing this, we are to meditate in what security and glorious contentment we shall enjoy the embraces of our Redeemer; seeing his bed and place for

OF THE CHURCH.

entertainment of the daughters of Jerusalem (that is, the souls of the faithful) is so excellently built and furnished, as this allegory implieth.

SONG XII.

Sing this as the Fifth Song.

1.

WHAT'S he, that from the desert, there,
    Doth like those smoky pillars come,
Which from the incense and the myrrh,
And all the merchant spices fume?
His bed (which, lo, is Solomon's)
Threescore stout men about it stand;
They are of Israel's valiant ones,
And all of them with swords in hand.

2.

All those are men expert in fight,
And each man on his thigh doth wear
A sword, that terrors of the night
May be forbid from coming there,
King Solomon a goodly place,
With trees of Lebanon, did rear;
Each pillar of it silver was,
And gold the bases of them were.

8.

With purple covered he the same,
And all the pavement (thoroughout)
Oh, Daughters of Jerusalem!
For you, with charity is wrought.
Come, Sion* Daughters, come away;
And crowned with his diadem,
King Solomon behold you may.
That crown his mother set on him,
When he a married man was made,
And at his heart contentment had.

THE FIFTH CANTICLE.

THAT loveliness which is found in the most beautiful body, endowed with the riches of the mind, and adorned with the goods of fortune (being of all objects the most powerful over human affections), the Holy Ghost, in this Song of Songs hath thereby mystically expressed the Church's estate in her several ages; that so it might the better work into our souls an apprehension both of those excellent perfections Christ hath bestowed on his church, and the better inform us also of that unspeakable

* The original reads " Come Syon Daughters."

affection which he bareth unto her. And it seemeth (the metaphors in this allegory being expounded), that the state of the Church, in her several members, is here described; with her lover's affection shewed towards her, about the time of the gospel's entrance, even when our blessed Saviour was abiding on the earth. But the explanation of each several metaphor will be too large for this place. Nor will every capacity reach unto the particular application of them. It may suffice, therefore, if such do (by an implicit faith) sing these mysteries with a general application of them to Christ and his Church, believing themselves members of that spouse; and that Jesus Christ is he, who in this Song professeth an entire affection, not only to the whole mystical body of the faithful, but even to every member of it in particular.

SONG XIII.

1.

OH, my Love! how comely now,
    And how beautiful art thou!
Thou of dove-like eyes a pair
Shining hast within thy hair.
And thy locks like kidlings be,
Which from Gilead Hill we see.

2.

Like those ewes thy teeth do show,
Which in rows from washing go,
When among them there is none
Twinless, nor a barren one.
And thy lips are of a red,
Like the rosy coloured thread.

3.

Speech becoming thee thou hast;
Underneath thy tresses plac'd,
Are thy temples (matchless fair)
Which, o'ershadow'd with thy hair,
Like pomegranates do appear,
When they cut asunder are.

4.

To that fort thy neck's compar'd,
Which with bulwarks David rear'd,
Where a thousand shields are hung,
All the targets of the strong.
Breasts thou hast, liked twinned roes,
Feeding where the lily grows.

5.

While day-break, and shades are gone,
To the mountains I will run;

OF THE CHURCH. 55

To that hill, whence myrrh doth come,
And to that of Lebanon;
Thou, my love, all beauty art,
Spotless fair in ev'ry part.

6.

Come, my spouse, from Lebanon,
Come with me from Lebanon,
From Amana turn thy sight,
Shenir's top, and Herman's height;
From the dens of lions fell,*
And the hills where leopards dwell.

7.

Thou, my sister, thou art she,
Of my heart that robbeth me;
Thou, my spouse, oh, thou art she,
Of my heart that robbeth me;
With one of thine eyes aspect,
And with one lock of thy neck.

8.

Sister, and espoused peer,
Those, thy breasts, how fair they are!
Better be those dugs of thine,
Than the most delicious wine;

* Fierce.

And thine ointments odours are
Sweeter than all spices far.

9.

Love, thy lips drop sweetness so,
As the combs of honey do;
Thou hast underneath thy tongue
Honey mixt with milk among;
And thy robes do scent as well
As the frankincense doth smell.

10.

Thou, my sister and espous'd,
Art a garden, fast enclos'd;
Walled-spring, a fountain seal'd;
And the plants thy orchard yield
Are of the pomegranate tree,
With those fruits that pleasant be.

11.

Camphor, there, with nard doth grow,
Nard commix'd with crocus too;
Calamus, and cinnamon,
With all trees, of Lebanon;
Sweetest aloes, and myrrh,
And all spice that precious are.

12.

All the gardens ev'ry where
Take their first beginning there:
There the precious fountain lies,
Whence all living waters rise;
Even all those streams that come
Running down from Lebanon.

THE SIXTH CANTICLE.

IN this Canticle is mystically set forth the death and passion of Jesus Christ; from whence all the sacraments and spiritual graces bestowed on the Church took their beginning. First, Christ desireth that, by the blowing of those two contrary winds, the charitable will of God, and the malicious will of his adversaries, the work of our redemption might be wrought: to which purpose the Church also addeth her request. Secondly, Christ sheweth, that he hath accomplished his own * with the Church's desire therein; and (expressing the fulfilling of his bitter-sweet passion) inviteth all the faithful to come and take benefit thereof. Thirdly, here is wondrous † movingly intimated, both our Redeemer's watchfulness to

* Original. " Accomplished his own."
† Original. " Wondrous movingly "

secure us (even while he slept in the grave), and those love passages of his, wherewith he came to woo us in his human nature (as it were a lover knocking and calling at his beloved's window) in the dark night of his passion, and unheeded afflictions. Lastly, here is described the Church's readiness to open to his Beloved; with that love distemperature, which appeared in her, when the women and the disciples missed him in the grave; and when, through fear of the high priests, they were for a time spoiled of their robe and veil of faith. This Canticle may properly be sung in commemoration of our Redeemer's sufferings, and of his Spouse's fear and sorrow before his Resurrection.

SONG XIV.

1.

ARISE, thou north wind, from the north,
And from the south, thou southwind blow;
Upon my garden breathe ye forth,
That so my spices (there that grow)
From thence abundantly may flow:
And to thy garden come, my dear,
To eat the fruits of pleasure there.

2.

My sister and espoused peer,
Unto my garden I am come;

OF THE CHURCH.

My spice I gather'd with my myrrh,
I ate my honey in the comb,
And drunk my wine with milk among ;
Come friends, and best belov'd of me,
Come eat and drink, and merry be.

3.

I slept, but yet my heart did wake ;
It is my love I knocking hear ;
It was his voice, and thus he spake,
Come, open unto me, my dear,
My love, my dove, my spotless peer ;
For with the dew my head is dight,*
My locks with droppings of the night.

4.

Lo, I have now undressed me,
Why should I clothe me as before ?
And since my feet clean washed be,
Why should I soil them any more ?
Then through the crevice of the door
Appear'd the hand of my belov'd,
And towards him my heart was mov'd.

5.

I rose, unto my love to ope,
And from my hands distilled myrrh ;

* Adorned.

Pure myrrh did from my fingers drop
Upon the handles of the bar;
But then departed was my dear.
When by his voice I knew 'twas he,
My heart was like to faint in me.

6.

I sought, but seen he could not be;
I call'd, but heard no answer sound.
The city watchmen met with me,
As they were walking of the round,
And gave me stripes that made a wound:
Yea, they that watch and ward the wall,
E'en they have took away my veil.

THE SEVENTH CANTICLE.

HERE is allegorically expressed the majesty, power, and excellency of Christ; and is the effect of that which was evangelically sung of him after his Resurrection and Ascension. First, the bride is introduced adjuring the faithful Israelites, that when they have attained the knowledge of Christ, her spouse, they should profess and teach him to the rest of their members. Secondly, those who long to find him, desire again of the Church to know the excellencies of that beloved of hers; and (by doubling the question) seem to imply a two-fold excellency. Thirdly, the Church speedily answers those that inquire after her spouse; and by describing his excellency (in his ten principal members) mystically notifieth his ten-fold spiritual perfection; whereupon to insist were not here convenient; Lastly, the faithful crave the Church's direction to help her find him out; and receive her gracious answer to that purpose.

SONG XV.

Sing this as the Thirteenth Song.

1.

OH! if him you happen on,
   Who is my beloved-one,
Daughters of Jerusalem,
I adjure you seriously
To inform him how that I
Sick am grown of love for him.

2.

Fairest of all women, tell
How thy lover doth excel,
More than other lovers do.
Thy beloved, what is he,
More than other lovers be;
That thou dost adjure us so?

3.

He in whom I so delight,
Is the purest red and white;
Of ten thousands chief is he;
Like fine gold his head doth show,
Whereon curled locks do grow;
And a raven-black they be.

4.

Like the milky doves that bide
By the rivers, he is ey'd:
Full and fitly set they are:
Cheeks like spicy-beds hath he;
Or like flowers that fairest be:
Lips like lilies dropping myrrh.

5.

Hands like rings of gold, beset
With the precious chrysolet;
Belly'd like white ivory,
Wrought about with sapphires rich;
Legs like marble pillars, which
Set on golden bases be.

6.

Fac'd like Libanus is he,
Goodly as the cedar tree,

Sweetness breathing out of him:
He is lovely ev'ry where.
This, my friend is, this my dear,
Daughters of Jerusalem.

7.

Oh, thou fairest (ev'ry way)
Of all women! whither may
Thy beloved turned be?
Tell us whither he is gone?*
Who is thy-beloved one,
That we seek him may with thee?

8.

To his garden went my dear,
To the beds of spices there;
Where he feeds, and lilies gets:
I my love's am, and (alone)
Mine is my beloved-one,
Who among the lilies eats.

* Whither is he gone?
What accident hath wrapt him from us?
Par. Regained.

THE EIGHTH CANTICLE.

HEREIN is contained a continuation of the praises of the Bride, and of that ardent affection expressed by her Beloved in the fifth Canticle; yet it is no unnecessary repetition: for it seemeth to have respect to the Church's estate, and the passages between her and Christ in another age; even when the Gentiles began to be called and united unto the church of the Jews, according to what is desired in the first Canticle: and therefore she is here compared to Tyrzah and Jerusalem for loveliness. Her glorious increase, her singular purity, her extraordinary applause, the splendour of her majesty, and the powerfulness of her authority, is here also described. Moreover, the fears and hinderances sustained in her first persecutions are here mystically shewn. And, lastly, they who through fear or obstinacy are separated from her, are called to return, in regard of her apparent power. This we may sing to remember us of those graces God hath bestowed on his Church. To comfort our souls, also, with that dearness which Christ expresseth towards her of whom we are members, and on divers other occasions, according as he that useth it hath capacity to understand and apply the same.

SONG XVI.

Sing this as the Thirteenth Song.

1.

BEAUTIFUL art thou my dear!
Thou as lovely art as are
Tirzah or Jerusalem,
(As the beautiful'st of them,)
And as much thou mak'st afraid,
As arm'd troops with flags display'd.

2.

Turn away those eyes of thine;
Do not fix them so on mine
For there beam forth (from thy sight)
Sweets that overcome me quite:
And thy locks like kidlings be,
Which from Gilead-hill we see.

8.

Like those ewes thy teeth do show,
Which in rows from washing go;
When among them there is none
Twinless, nor a barren one.
And (within thy locks) thy brows
Like the cut pomegranate shows.

4.

There are with her sixty queens :
There are eighty concubines ;
And the damsels they possess
Are in number numberless :
But my dove is all alone,
And an undefiled one.

5.

She's her mother's only dear,
And her joy that did her bear ;
When the daughters her survey'd,
That she blessed was they said :
She was praised of the queens.
And among the concubines.

6.

Who is she (when forth she goes)
That so like the morning shows ?
Beautiful, as is the moon ;
Purely bright, as is the sun ;
And appearing full of dread,
Like an host with ensigns spread !

7.

To the nut-yard down went I,
(And the vale's increase to spy)

To behold the vine-buds come,
And to see pomegranates bloom;
But the prince's chariots did
Vex me so, I could not heed.

8.

Turn, oh turn, thou Shulamite!
Turn, oh turn thee to our sight!
What I pray, is that which you
In the Shulamite would view,
But that (to appearance) she
Shews like troops that armed be.

THE NINTH CANTICLE.

SOLOMON, in the first part of this Canticle, commending the Church's universal beauty in her several parts, is understood to have respect to that time after the conversion from Paganism, wherein she was endowed and made lovely by the variety of those offices, states, and degrees, into which her members were for order's sake distinguished; as well as by the addition of those other graces formally received: which states and degrees are here mystically understood by the parts of a beautiful woman (as doth excellently appear, the allegory being particularly expounded.) The second part of this Hymn expresseth the mutual interchange of affections between the Bridegroom and his bride; and those sweet contentments they enjoy in each other's loves. Lastly, here is set forth both the Church's desire to be freed from those persecutions, which hinder her open and full fruition of her beloved; and mention is here made also of those public and undisturbed embraces which they shall at length enjoy. The first part hereof we ought so to sing, that it may remember us to shun their blindness, who discern not the beauty of order and degrees in the Church. The second part puts us in mind that she is the treasuress both of those graces which cause contentment within ourselves, and make us acceptable to God. By the last part we may apprehend the comfort that will follow, when we desire that the open profession of Christ may be granted merely for the love of him.

SONG XVII.

Sing this as the Ninth Song.

1.

THOU daughter of the royal line,*
How comely are those feet of thine,
When their beseeching shoes they wear!

* Weep, daughter of a Royal line!—*Byron.*

OF THE CHURCH.

The curious knittings of thy thighs
Is like the costly gems of prize,
Which wrought by skilful workmen are.

2.

Thy navel is a goblet crown'd,
Where liquor evermore is found;
Thy fair and fruitful belly shows,
As doth a goodly heap of wheat,
With lilies round about beset,
And thy two breasts like twinned roes.

3.

Thy neck like some white tower doth rise;
Like Heshbon fish-pools are thine eyes,
Which near the gate Bath-rabbim lie.
Thy nose (which thee doth well become)
Is like the tower of Libanum,
That on Damascus hath an eye.

4.

Thy head like scarlet doth appear;
The hairs thereof like purple are;
And in those threads the King is bound.
Oh, Love! how wondrous fair art thou!
How perfect do thy pleasures show!
And how their joys in them abound!

5.

Thou statured* art in palm-tree wise;
Thy breasts like clusters do arise :
I said unto this palm I'll go,
My hold shall on her branches be ;
And those thy breasts shall be to me
Like clusters that on vines do grow.

6.

Thy nostrils savour shall as well
As newly gathered fruits do smell,
Thy speech shall also relish so,
As purest wine, that for my dear
As fitting drink, and able were
To cause an old man's lips to go.

7.

I my beloved's am, and he
Hath his affection set on me.
Come, well-beloved, come away,
Into the fields let's walk along ;
And there the villages among,
E'en in the country we will stay.

8.

We to the vines betimes will go,
And see if they do spring or no ;

* Like a Statue.

Or, if the tender grapes appear:
We will, moreover, go and see
If the pomegranates blossom'd be;
And I my love will give thee there.

9.

Sweet smells the mandrakes do afford,
And we within our gates are stor'd,
Of all things that delightful be:
Yea, whether new or old they are,
Prepared they be for my dear,
And I have laid them up for thee.

10.

Would as my brother thou might'st be,
That suck'd my mother's breast with me;
Oh, would it were no otherwise!
In public then I thee would meet,
And give thee kisses in the street,
And none there is should thee despise.

11.

Then I myself would for thee come,
And bring thee to my mother's home;
Thou likewise should'st instruct me there;
And wine that is commixt with spice
(Sweet wine of the pomegranate juice)
I would for thee to drink prepare.

12.

My head with his left hand he staid ;
His right hand over me he laid ;
And being so embrac'd by him,
Said he, I charge you, not disease,
· Nor wake my love, until she please,
You daughters of Jerusalem.

THE TENTH CANTICLE.

IN this last part of Solomon's Song he first singeth that sweet peace and extraordinary prosperity vouchsafed unto the Church after her great persecutions; and expresseth it by putting the question, who she was that came out of the wilderness leaning on her Beloved. Secondly, he introduceth Christ putting the human nature in remembrance from what estate he had raised it, and requiring the dearest of our affections, in regard of the ardency, unquenchableness, and inestimable value of his love. Thirdly, having remembered the Church of the affection due to him, Christ teacheth her the charitable care she ought to have of others; and that she being brought into his favour and protection, should seek the preferment of her younger sister also, even the

OF THE CHURCH. 73

people who have not yet the breasts of God's two testaments to nourish their souls. Fourthly, the Church's true Solomon, or Peace-Maker (meaning Jesus Christ) having a vineyard in Baal-hammon (that is) wheresoever there are people; herein is declared the reward of such as are profitably employed in that vineyard. And lastly, the confirmation of Christ's marriage upon the hills of spice (meaning Heaven) is hastened. In singing this Canticle we ought to meditate what estate God hath raised us from; what love he hath vouchsafed; what our charity should be to others; what we should mind concerning this life, and what desire we should have to the comforts of the world to come.

SONG XVIII.

1.

WHO'S this, that leaning on her friend,
  Doth from the wilderness ascend?
Mind how I raised thee,
E'en where thy mother thee conceiv'd,
Where she that brought thee forth conceiv'd,
  Beneath an apple-tree.

2.

Me in thy heart engraven bear,
And seal-like on thy hand-wrist wear

For love is strong as death ;
Fierce as the grave is Jealousy,
The coals thereof do burning lie,
And furious flames it hath.

3.

Much water cannot cool love's flame,
No floods have power to quench the same,
For love so high is priz'd,
That who to buy it would essay,
Though all his wealth he gave away,
It would be all despis'd.

4.

We have a sister, scarcely grown,
For she is such a little one,
That yet no breasts hath she ;
What things shall we now undertake
To do for this our sister's sake,
If spoken for she be ?

5.

If that a wall she do appear,
We turrets upon her will rear,
And palaces of plate :
And then with boards of cedar-tree
Enclose, and fence her in will we,
If that she be a gate.

6.

A wall already built I am,
And now my breasts upon the same,
  Do turret-like arise;
Since when, as one that findeth rest,
(And is of settled peace possest)
  I seemed in his eyes.

7.

A vineyard hath King Solomon,
This vineyard is at Baal-hammon,
  Which he to keepers put;
And ev'ry one that therein wrought,
A thousand silver-pieces brought,
  And gave him for the fruit.

8.

My vineyard, which belongs to me,
E'en I myself do oversee:
  To thee, O Solomon,
A thousand-fold doth appertain,
And those that keep the same shall gain
  Two hundred-fold for one.

9.

Thou whose abode the gardens are,
(Thy fellows unto thee give ear)

Cause me to hear thy voice:
And let my Love as swiftly go,
As doth a hart or nimble roe,
Upon the hills of spice.

THE FIRST SONG OF ESAI.

Esa. v.

IN this Song the Prophet, singing of Christ and his vineyard, first sheweth, that, notwithstanding his labour bestowed in fencing and manuring thereof it brought forth sour grapes. Secondly, he summoneth their consciences whom he covertly upbraided, to be judges of God's great love, and their unprofitableness. Thirdly, he shows both how he intends to deal with his vineyard, and who they are whom he pointeth out in this parable. Now, seeing it hath befallen the Jews according to this prophetical hymn, we are to make a twofold use in singing it. First, thereby to memorize the mercy and justice of God, both which are manifested in this song: his mercy in forewarning, his justice in punishing even his own people. Secondly, we are so to meditate thereon, that we may be warned to consider what favours God hath vouchsafed us, and what fruits we ought to bring forth; lest he leave us also to be spoiled of our adversaries: for in this parable the Holy Spirit speaketh unto every congregation who abuseth his favours. And doubtless all such (as it hath fallen out in Antioch, Laodicea, and many other particular churches) shall be deprived of God's protection, of the dews of his Holy Spirit, and of the sweet showers of his word, to be left to thorns and briers, the fruit of their natural corruptions.

SONG XIX.

Sing this as the Fourteenth Song.

1.

A SONG of Him whom I love best,
And of his Vineyard sing I will.
A vineyard once my love possest,
Well-seated on a fruitful hill;
He kept it close-immured still:
The earth from stones he did refine,
And set it with the choicest vine.

2.

He in the midst a fort did rear.
(A wine-press therein also wrought;)
But when he look'd it grapes should bear,
Those grapes were wild ones that it brought.
Jerusalem, come speak thy thought,

And you of Judah judges be,
Betwixt my vineyards here, and me.

3.

Unto my vineyard what could more
Performed be, than I have done?
Yet looking it should grapes have bore,
Save wild ones it afforded none.
But go to, (let it now alone)
Resolv'd I am to shew you too,
What with my vineyard I will do.

4.

The hedge I will remove from thence,
That what so will, devour it may.
I down will break the walled-fence,
And through it make a trodden way.
Yea, all of it I waste will lay.
To dig or dress it none shall care :
But thorns and briers it shall bear.

5.

The clouds I also will compel,
That there no rain descend for this ;
For lo the house of Israel
The Lord of Armies' vineyard is :
And Judah is that plant of his,

That pleasant one, who forth has brought
Oppression, when he judgment sought.
He seeking justice, found therein,
In lieu thereof, a crying sin.

THE SECOND SONG OF ESAI.

Esai xii.

ISAIAH having a little before prophesied of the Incarnation of Jesus Christ, and the excellency of his kingdom, doth in this Hymn praise him for his mercy; and foreshows the Church also, what her Song should be in that day of her redemption, the principal contents whereof are these: A confession of God's mercy, a prediction concerning the sacrament of baptism, and an exhortation to a joyful thanksgiving. This Song the Church should still sing to the honour of Jesus Christ for our redemption. Yea, in regard to the Prophet (foreseeing the good cause we should have to make use hereof) hath prophesied it should be the Church's Hymn, it seemeth not improper to be used on those days, which are solemnized in memorial of our Saviour's Nativity; or whensoever we shall be moved to praise God, in memorizing the gracious comforts promised us by his Prophets, and fulfilled by his own coming. And to fit the same the better to that purpose, I have changed the person and the time in this translation.

SONG XX.

1.

LORD, I will sing to Thee,
 For thou displeased wast,
And yet withdrew'st thy wrath from me,
And sent me comfort hast.
Thou art my health, on whom
A fearless trust I lay:
For thou, oh Lord! thou art become
My strength, my song, my stay!

2.

And with rejoicing now,
Sweet waters we convey,
Forth of those springs whence life doth flow;
And, thus, we therefore say,
Oh, sing unto the Lord;
His name and works proclaim;
Yea, to the people bear record
That glorious is his name.

8.

Unto the Lord, oh sing,
For wonders he hath done,
And many a renowned thing,
Which through the earth is known.
Oh sing aloud, all ye
On Sion-hill that dwell;
For, lo, thy Holy One in thee
Is great, oh Israel!

THE THIRD SONG OF ESAI.

Esai xxvi.

ESAI composed this Song to comfort the Israelites in their captivity; to strengthen their patience in affliction and settle their confidence on the promises of God. First, it remembereth them that God's protection being everywhere as available as a defenced city, they ought always to rely on the firm peace which that affordeth. Secondly, he sheweth that the pride of sin shall be overthrown; and that the faithful are resolved to fly unto their Redeemer, and await his pleasure in their chastisements. Thirdly, he singeth the utter desolation of tyrants; the increase of the Church; her afflictions; her deliverance and the resurrection from death through Christ. Lastly, the faithful are exhorted to attend patiently on the Lord their Saviour, who will come shortly to judgment, and take account for the blood of his saints. This Song is made in the person of the Church, and may be sung to comfort and confirm us in all our chastisements and persecutions; by bringing to our consideration the short time of our endurance, and the certainty of our Redeemer's coming. It may be used also to praise God both for his justice and mercy.

SONG XXI.

Sing this as the Third Song.

1.

A CITY now we have obtain'd,
Where strong defences are;
And God salvation hath ordain'd
For walls and bulwarks there.
The gates thereof wide open ye,
That such as justly do,
(And those that Truth's observers be)
May enter thereunto.

2.

There thou in peace wilt keep them sure,
Whose thoughts well grounded be;

OF THE CHURCH.

In peace that ever shall endure,
Because they trusted Thee.
For ever, therefore, on the Lord,
Without distrust, depend;
For in the Lord, th' eternal Lord,
Is strength that hath no end.

3.

He makes the lofty city yield,
And her proud dwellers bow;
He lays it level with the field,
E'en with the dust below.
Their feet that are in want and care,
Their feet thereon shall tread;
Their way is right, that righteous are,
And thou their path dost heed.

4.

Upon the course of judgments we,
Oh, Lord, attending were,
And to record thy name and thee,
Our souls desirous are.
On thee our minds, with strong desire,
Are fixed in the night;
And after thee our hearts inquire,
Before the morning light.

5.

For when thy righteous judgments are
Upon the earth discern'd,
By those that do inhabit there,
Uprightness shall be learn'd.
Yet sinners for no terror will
Just dealing understand,
But in their sins continue still,
Amid the Holy Land.

6.

To seek the glory of the Lord
They unregardful be;
And thy advanced hand, oh Lord,
They will not deign to see.
But they shall see, and see with shame,
That bear thy people spite;
Yea, from thy foes shall come a flame,
Which will devour them quite.

7.

Then, Lord, for us thou wilt procure
That we in peace may be,
Because that every work of our
Is wrought for us by thee.
And, Lord our God, though we are brought
To other lords in thrall,
Of thee alone shall be our thought,
Upon thy name to call.

OF THE CHURCH.

8.

They are deceas'd, and never shall
Renewed life obtain;
They die, and shall not rise at all
To tyrannise again:
For thou didst visit them, therefore,
And wide dispers'd them hast;
That so their fame for evermore
May wholly be defac'd.

9.

But, Lord, increas'd thy people are,
Increas'd they are by thee;
And thou art glorified as far
As earth's wide limits be;
For, Lord, in their distresses, when
Thy rod on them was laid,
They unto thee did hasten then,
And without ceasing pray'd.

10.

As one with child is pained, when as
Her throes of bearing be,
And cries in pangs (before thy face;)
O Lord, so fared we.
We have conceiv'd, and for a birth
Of wind have pained been.
The world's unsafe, and still on earth
They thrive that dwell therein.

11.

The dead shall live, and rise again
With my dead body shall.
Oh, you, that in the dust remain,
Awake, and sing you all!
For as the dew doth herbs renew,
That buried seem'd before,
So earth shall through thy heavenly dew
Her dead to life restore.

12.

My people, to thy chambers fair;
Shut close the door to thee,
And stay a while (a moment there)
Till past the fury be:
For lo, the Lord doth now arise,
He cometh from his place,
To punish their impieties,
Who now the world possess.

13.

The earth that blood discover shall
Which is in her concealed,
And bring to light those murders all
Which yet are unrevealed.

The edit. of 1623 has the above stanza with only four lines.

THE PRAYER OF HEZEKIAH.

Esai. xxxvii., 15.

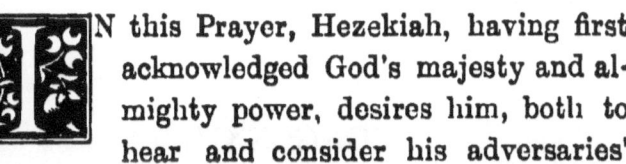N this Prayer, Hezekiah, having first acknowledged God's majesty and almighty power, desires him, both to hear and consider his adversaries' blasphemy: then (to manifest the necessity of his present assistance) urgeth the power his foe had obtained over such as served not the true God: and as it seemeth, importunes deliverance, not so much in regard of his own safety, as that the blasphemer, and all the world might know the difference between the Lord's power, and the arrogant brags of men. This song may be used whensoever the Turk, or any other great adversary (prevailing against false worshippers) shall thereupon grow insolent, and threaten God's Church also; as if, in despite of him he had formerly prevailed by his own strength. For the name of Sennacherib may be mystically applied to any such enemy. We may use this hymn also against those secret blasphemies which the Devil whispers unto our souls; or when by temptations he seeks to drive us to despair, by laying before us

how many others he hath destroyed, who seemed to have been in as good assurance as we; for he is indeed that mystical Assyrian Prince, who hath overthrown whole countries and nations, with their gods in whom they trusted. Such as are these, temporal power, riches, superstitious worship, carnal wisdom, idols, etc., which being but the works of men (and yet trusted in as gods), he hath power to destroy them.

SONG XXII.

1.

O LORD of Hosts, and God of Israel!
    Thou who between the Cherubims dost dwell;
Of all the world thou only art the King,
And heaven and earth unto their form didst bring.

2.

Lord, bow thine ear; to hear attentive be;
Lift up thine eyes, and deign, O Lord, to see
What words Sennacherib hath cast abroad,
And his proud message to the living God!

3.

Lord, true it is, that lands and kingdoms all
Are to the king of Ashur brought in thrall;

Yea, he their gods into the fire hath thrown,
For gods they were not, but of wood and stone.

4.

Man's work they were, and men destroy'd them have;
Us, therefore, from his power vouchsafe to save,
That all the kingdoms of the world may see
That thou art God, that only thou art he.

HEZEKIAH'S THANKSGIVING.

Esai. xxxviii. 10.

EZEKIAH, having been sick, and recovered, made this Song of Thanksgiving; and setteth forth the mercy of God, by considering these particulars: The time of his age; the fears of his soul; the rooting out of his posterity; the violence of his disease; and the forgiveness of his sins, added to the restoring of his health. Then (seeming to have entered into a serious consideration of all this) he confesseth who are most bound to praise God, and voweth this deliverance to everlasting memory. This Song may be used after deliverance from temporal sickness. But, in the principal sense, it is a special Thanksgiving for

that cure which Jesus Christ wrought upon the human nature, being in danger of everlasting perdition: for Hezekiah which signifieth *helped of the Lord*, typifieth mankind labouring under the sickness of sin and death. Isaiah, who brought the medicine that cured him (and is interpreted the *Salvation of the Lord*), figured our blessed Redeemer, by whom the human nature is restored; and whose sending into the world was mystically shewed by the miracle of the sun's retrogadation. To praise God for that mystery therefore (the circumstances being well considered), this Hymn seemeth very proper. And doubtless for this cause it was partly preserved for these our times, and ought often and heartily to be sung to that purpose.

SONG XXIII.

Sing this as the Fourth Song

1.

WHEN I suppos'd my time was at an end,
    Thus to myself I did myself bemoan :
Now to the gates of hell I must descend,
For all the remnant of my years are gone.
The Lord (said I) where now the living be,
Nor man on earth shall I for ever see.

2.

As when a shepherd hath remov'd his tent,
Or as a weaver's shuttle slips away,
Right so my dwelling and my years were spent;
And so my sickness did my life decay;
Each day, ere night, my death expected;
And every night, ere morning, thought to die.

3.

For he, so lion-like, my bones did break,
That I scarce thought to live another day :
A noise I did like cranes or swallows make,
And, as the turtle I lamenting lay.
Then with uplifted eye-lids, thus I spake,
Oh Lord, on me oppressed, mercy take !

4.

What shall I say ? he did his promise give,
And as he promis'd he performed it;
And, therefore, I will never, whilst I live,
Those bitter passions of my soul forget:
Yea, those that live, and those unborn, shall know
What life and rest thou didst on me bestow.

5.

My former pleasures sorrows were become ;
But in that love which to my soul thou hast,

The grave, that all devours, thou keepst me from,
And didst my errors all behind thee cast;
For, nor the grave, nor death can honour thee;
Nor hope they for thy truth that buried be.

6.

Oh; he that lives, that lives as I do now,
E'en he it is that shall thy praise declare;
Thy truth the father to his seed shall shew.
And how thou me, oh Lord hast deigned to spare!
Yea, Lord, for this I will throughout my days,
Make music in thy house unto thy praise.

THE LAMENTATIONS OF EREMIAH.

AS useful as any part of the Old Testament, for these present times (nigh fallen asleep in security) are these Elegical Odes; for they bring many things to our consideration. First, what we may and should lament for. Secondly, how careful we ought to be of the common-wealth's prosperity; because, if that go to ruin, the particular Church therein cherished must needs be afflicted also, and God's worship hindered. Thirdly, they teach us, that the overthrow of kingdoms and empires follows the abuse and neglect of religion: and that (sin being the only cause thereof) we ought to endure our chastisements without murmuring against God. Fourthly, they warn us not to abuse God's merciful long-suffering. Fifthly, they persuade us to commiserate and pray for the Church and our brethren in calamities, and not to despise them in their humiliations. Sixthly, they leave us not to judge the truth of professions, by those afflictions God lays upon particular churches, seeing the Jewish religion was the truth, and those idolaters, who led them into captivity. Seventhly, they shew us, that neither the antiquity, strength, fame, or formal sanctity of any place (no, nor God's former respect thereunto) shall privilege it from destruction, if it continue in abusing his grace. And, lastly, they (as it were, limiting our sorrows) mind us to cast our eyes on the mercies of God; and to make such use of his chastisements, as may turn our lamentations into songs of joy.

LAMENT. I.

THIS Elegy first bewaileth, in general terms, that calamity and destruction of Judah and Jerusalem, which is afterwards more particularly mentioned. Secondly, it makes a confession of their manifold sins committed; and is full of many passionate and pentitential complaints, justifying the Lord in his judgments, and confessing the vanity of human consolations. Lastly, it containeth a short prayer for God's mercy, and a divine prediction of those judgments which will fall on them, by whom his people have been afflicted. This Elegy may be sung whensoever any general calamity falleth on the commonwealth in which we live; we having first considered and applied the particular circumstances, as there shall be cause. We may sing it also *historically*, to memorize the justice of God, and the miserable desolations of Judah and Jerusalem, recorded for our example.

SONG XXIV.

1.

HOW sad and solitary now (alas!)
    Is that well-peopled city come to be,
Which once so great among the nations was!
And, oh, how widow-like appeareth she!
She rule of all the provinces hath had,
And now herself is tributary made!

2.

All night she maketh such excessive moan,
That down her cheeks a flood of tears doth flow!

And yet among her lovers there is none
That consolation doth on her bestow !
For they that once her lovers did appear,
Now turned foes, and faithless to her are !

3.

Now Judah in captivity complains
That (others) heretofore so much opprest,
For her false service, she herself remains
Among those heathens, where she finds no rest.
And apprehended in a strait is she,
By those that persecutors of her be !

4.

The very ways of Sion do lament;
The gates thereof their loneliness deplore;
Because that no man cometh to frequent
Her solemn festivals, as heretofore.
Her priests do sigh, her tender virgins be
Uncomfortable left, and so is she !

5.

Her adversaries are become her chiefs;
On high exalted, those that hate her are;
And God hath brought upon her all those griefs,
Because so many her transgressions were.
Her children, driven from her by the foe,
Before him into loathed thraldom go.

6.

From Sion's daughters (once without compare)
Now all her matchless loveliness is gone:
And like those chased harts, her princes fair,
Who seek for pasture, and can find out none.
So (of their strength depriv'd and fainting nigh)
Before their abler foes they feebly fly.

7.

Jerusalem now thinks upon her crimes,
And calls to mind (amid her present woes)
The pleasure she enjoy'd in former times,
Till first she was surprised by her foes:
And how (when they perceived her forlorn)
They at her holy sabbaths made a scorn.

8.

Jerusalem's transgressions many were;
And therefore is it she disdained lies:
Those who in former time have honour'd her,
Her baseness now behold, and her despise.
Yea, she herself doth sit bewailing this,
And of herself herself ashamed is.

9.

Her own uncleanness in her skirt she bore,
Not then believing what her end would be:

This great destruction falls on her therefore,
And none to help or comfort her hath she.
Oh, heed thou, Lord! and pity thou my woes,
For I am triumph'd over by my foes!

10.

Her foe hath touch'd with his polluted hand
Her things that sacred were, before her face:
And they whose entrance thou didst countermand,
Intruded have into her holy place:
Those, that were not so much approv'd by thee,
As of thy congregation held to be.

11.

Her people do, with sighs and sorrows, get
That little bread, which for relief they have:
And give away their precious things for meat.
So to procure wherewith their life to save:
Oh, Lord! consider this, and ponder thou,
How vile and how dejected I am now:

12.

No pity in you, passengers, is there?
Your eyes, oh! somewhat hitherward incline;
And mark, if ever any grief there were,
Or sorrow that did equal this of mine!'
This which the Lord on me inflicted hath,
Upon the day of his incensed wrath.

H

13.

He from above a flame hath hurled down,
That kindles in my bones prevailing fire :
A net he over both my feet hath thrown,
By which I am compelled to retire.
And he hath made me a forsaken one,
To sit and weep out all the day alone.

14.

The heavy yoke of my transgressions now
His hand hath wreathed, and upon me laid;
Beneath the same my tired neck doth bow,
And all my strength is totally decay'd.
For me to those the Lord hath given o'er,
Whose hands will hold me fast for evermore.

15.

The Lord hath trampled underneath their feet
E'en all the mighty in the midst of me :
A great assembly he hath caus'd to meet,
That all my ablest men might slaughter'd be ;
And Judah's virgin daughter treads upon,
As in a wine-press grapes are trodden on.

16.

For this (alas!) thus weep I; and mine eyes,
Mine eyes drop water thus, because that he,
On whose assistance my sad soul relies,

OF THE CHURCH.

In my distress is far away from me :
E'en while (because of my prevailing foe)
My children are compell'd from me to go.

17.

In vain hath Sion stretched forth her hand,
For none unto her succour draweth nigh;
Because the Lord hath given in command,
That Jacob's foes should round about her lie:
And poor Jerusalem, among them there,
Like some defiled woman doth appear.

18.

The Lord is justified, nay-the-less,*
Because I did not his commands obey;
All nations, therefore, hear my heaviness,
And heed it (for your warning) you, I pray;
For into thraldom (through my follies) be
My virgins, and my young men, borne from me.

19.

Upon my lovers I have cried out ;
But they my groundless hopes deceived all:
I for my rev'rend priests inquir'd about;
I, also, did upon my elders call ;
But in the city up the ghost they gave,
As they were seeking meat, their lives|to save.

* Nevertheless.

20.

Oh, Lord! take pity now in my distress;
For, lo, my soul distemper'd is in me;
My heart is overcome with heaviness,
Because I have so much offended thee!
Thy sword abroad, my ruin doth become,
And death doth also threaten me at home!

21.

And of my sad complaints my foes have heard;
But to afford me comfort there is none:
My troubles have at full to them appear'd,
Yet they are joyful that thou so hast done:
But thou wilt bring the time set down by thee,
And then in sorrow they shall equal me.

22.

Then shall those foul offences they have wrought
Before the presence be remembered all:
And whatsoe'er my sins on me have brought,
(For their transgressions) upon them shall fall:
For so my sighings multiplied be,
That, therewithal, my heart is faint in me.

LAMENT. II.

IN this Elegy the Prophet useth a very pathetical exordium, the better to awaken the people's consideration; and to make them the more sensible of their horrible calamity; which he first illustrateth in general terms, by comparing their estate to the miserable condition of one fallen from the glory of heaven to the lowest earth; and in mentioning their being deprived of that glorious temporal and ecclesiastical government, which they formerly enjoyed. Afterwards, he descends to particulars; as the destruction of their palaces, forts, temples, walls, and gates; the profaning of their sabbaths, feasts, rites, &c.; the suspending of their laws, priests, prophets; the slaughter of young men and virgins, old men and children; with the famine and reproaches they sustained, &c. All which acknowledging to be the just judgments of God, he adviseth them not to hearken to the delusions of their false prophets, but to return unto the Lord by tears and hearty repentance. For the use and application, see what hath been said, before the former Elegy.

SONG XXV.

Sing this as the Twenty-fourth Song.

1.

HOW dark, and how be-clouded (in his wrath)
The Lord hath caused Sion to appear!
How Israel's beauty he obscured hath,
As if thrown down from heav'n to earth he were!
Oh! why is his displeasure grown so hot?
And why hath he his footstool so forgot?

2.

The Lord all Sion's dwellings hath laid waste;
And, in so doing, he no sparing made:
For in his anger to the ground he cast
The strongest holds that Judah's daughter had.
Them, and their kingdom, he to ground doth send,
And all the Princes of it doth suspend.

3.

When at the highest his displeasure was,
From Israel all his horn of strength he broke;
And from before his adversary's face
His right-hand (that restrained him) he took,
Yea, he in Jacob kindled such a flame,
As, round about, hath quite consum'd the same.

4.

His bow he as an adversary bent,
And by his right-hand he did plainly shew
He drew it with an enemy's intent
For all that were the fairest marks he slew.
In Sion's tabernacle this was done;
E'en there the fire of his displeasure shone.

5.

The Lord himself is he that was the foe;
By him is Israel thus to ruin gone.
His palaces he overturned so;
And he his holds of strength hath overthrown:
E'en he it is, from whom it doth arise,
That Israel's daughter thus lamenting lies.

6.

His tabernacle, garden-like that was,
The Lord with violence hath took away:
He hath destroyed his assembling-place;
And there no feasts nor sabbaths now have they:
No, not in Sion; for in his fierce wrath
He both their King and Priests rejected hath!

7.

The Lord his holy altar doth forego;
His sanctuary he hath quite despis'd.

Yea, by his mere assistance hath our foe
The bulwarks of our palaces surpriz'd :
And in the Lord's own house rude noises are
As loud as heretofore his praises were.

8.

The Lord his thought did purposely incline,
The walls of Sion should be overthrown :
To that intent he stretched forth his line,
And drew not back his hand till they were down.
And so, the turrets, with the bruised wall,
Did both together to destruction fall.

9.

Her gates in heaps of earth obscured are ;
The bars of them in pieces broke hath he :
Her king, and those that once her princes were,
Now borne away among the Gentiles be.
The law is lost, and they no prophet have,
That from the Lord a vision doth receive.

10.

In silence, seated on the lowly ground,
The senators of Sion's daughter are :
With ashes they their careful heads have crown'd,
And mourning sackcloth girded on them wear.
Yea, on the earth in a distressed-wise,
Jerusalem's young virgins fix their eyes.

11.

And, for because my people suffer this,
Mine eyes with much lamenting dimmed grow ;
Each part within me out of quiet is,
And on the ground my liver forth I throw :
When as mine eyes with so sad objects meet,
As babes half dead, and sprawling in the street.

12.

For, to their mothers called they for meat ;
Oh where shall we have meat and drink ! they cry ;
And in the city, while they food entreat,
They swoon, like them that deadly wounded lie ;
And some of them their souls did breathe away,
As in the mother's bosom starv'd they lay.

13.

Jerusalem ! for thee what can I say ?
Or unto what may'st thou resembled be ?
Oh ! whereunto that comfort thee I may,
Thou Sion's daughter, shall I liken thee ?
For, as the seas, so great thy breaches are ;
And to repair them then, ah, who is there ?

14.

Thou by thy prophets has deluded been ;
And foolish visions they for thee have sought.

For, they revealed not to thee thy sin,
To turn away the thraldom it hath brought.
But lying prophecies they sought for thee,
Which of thy sad exile the causes be.

15.

And those, thou daughter of Jerusalem,
That on occasions pass along this way,
With clapping hands, and hissings, thee contemn;
And, nodding at thee, thus in scorn they say:
Is this the city men did once behight*
The flower of beauty, and the world's delight?

16.

Thy adversaries (everyone of them)
Their mouths have open'd at thee to thy shame;
They hiss, and gnash at thee, Jerusalem;
We, we (say they) have quite destroy'd the same;
This is that day hath long expected been;
Now cometh it, and we the same have seen.

17.

But, this the Lord decreed, and brought to pass;
He, to make good that word which once he spake,
(And that which long ago determin'd was)
Hath hurled down, and did no pity take.
He thus hath made thee scorned of thy foe,
And rais'd the horn of them that hate thee so.

* Or call.

18.

Oh wall of Sion's daughter, cry amain;
E'en to the Lord set forth a hearty cry:
Down, like a river, cause thy tears to rain,
And let them neither day nor night be dry.
Seek neither sleep, thy body to suffice,
Nor slumber for the apples of thine eyes.

19.

At night, and when the watch is new began,
Then rise, and to the Lord Almighty cry:
Before him let thy heart like water run,
And lift thou up to him thy hands on high.
E'en for those hunger-starved babes of thine,
That in the corners of the streets do pine.

20.

And thou, oh Lord, oh be thou pleas'd to see,
And think on whom thy judgments thou hast thrown!
Shall women fed with their own issue be,
And children that a span are scarcely grown?
Shall thus thy priests and prophets, Lord, be slain,
As in thy sanctuary they remain?

21.

Nor youth, nor age, is from the slaughter free;
For in the streets lie young, and old, and all.

My virgins and my young men murdered be ;
E'en both beneath the sword together fall.
Thou, in thy day of wrath, such havoc mad'st,
That in devouring thou no pity hadst.

22.

Thou round about hast call'd my feared foes,
As if that summon'd to some feast they were;
Who in thy day of wrath did round enclose,
And shut me so, that none escaped are.
Yea, those that hate me, them consumed have,
To whom I nourishment and breeding gave.

LAMENT. III.

HERE the Prophet Jeremy, having contemplated his own afflictions, with the destruction of Judah and Jerusalem, seemeth, by that material object, to have raised his apprehension higher, and, by the spirit of prophecy, both to foresee the particular sufferings of Jesus Christ, and to become sensible also of those great afflictions which the church militant (his mystical body) should be exercised withal. And in this most passionate Elegy, either in his own person bewaileth it, or else personates Jesus Christ, the head of that mystical body ;

taking upon himself those punishments, with that heavy burden of God's wrath, and that unspeakable sorrow, which mankind had otherwise been overwhelmed withal. In brief, this Elegy contains an expression of God's heavy anger for our sins; the severity and bitterness of his judgments; the greatness of his mercies; the hope and patience of the faithful in all afflictions; the unwillingness of God to punish; the hearty repentance of his people; and a prophetical imprecation concerning the enemies of the spiritual Jerusalem. This may be sung to move and stir us up with a feeling of our Redeemer's Passion; to remember us of our miserable condition through sin; to move us to repentance; and to comfort and instruct us amid our afflictions.

SONG XXVI.

Sing this as the Twenty-Fourth Song.

1.

I AM the man (who scourged in thy wrath)
Have in all sorrows throughly tried been:
Into obscurity he led me hath;
He brought me thither, where no light is seen;
And so adverse to me himself he shows,
That all the day his hand doth me oppose.

2.

My flesh and skin with age he tired out;
He bruis'd my bones, as they had broken been;
He with a wall enclosed me about,
With cares and labours he hath shut me in:
And me to such a place of darkness led,
As those are in, that be for ever dead.

3.

He shut me where I found no passage out,
And there my heavy chains upon me laid;
Moreover, though I loudly cried out,
He took no heed at all for what I pray'd:
My way with hewed stones he stopped hath,
And left me wand'ring in a winding path.

4.

He was to me like some way-laying bear;
Or as a lion that doth lurk unseen;
My course he hind'ring, me in pieces tare,
Till I quite ruin'd and laid waste had been.
His bow he bended, and that being bent,
I was the mark at which his arrow went.

5.

His arrows from his quiver forth he caught,
And through my very reins he made them pass:

E'en mine own people set me then at naught,
And all the day their sporting song I was.
From him my fill of bitterness I had,
And me with wormwood likewise drunk he made.

6.

With stones my teeth he all to pieces brake
He dust and ashes over me hath strown:
All rest he from my weary soul did take,
As if contentment I had never none.
And then I cried, Oh! I am undone!
All my dependance on the Lord is gone!

7.

Oh mind thou my afflictions and my care,
My miseries, my wormwood, and my gall;
For they still fresh in my remembrance are,
And down in me my humbled soul doth fall.
I this forget not; and when this I mind,
Some help again I do begin to find.

8.

It is thy mercy, Lord, that we now be,
For had thy pity fail'd not one had liv'd.
The faithfulness is great that is in thee,
And ev'ry morning it is new reviv'd:
And, Lord, such claim my soul unto thee lays,
That she will ever trust in thee, she says.

9.

For thou art kind to those that wait thy will,
And to their souls, that after thee attend:
Good therefore is it, that in quiet still,
We hope that safety, which thou, Lord, wilt send.
And happy he, that timely doth enure
His youthful neck the burden to endure.

10.

He down will sit alone, and nothing say;
But since 'tis cast upon him, bear it out:
(Yea, though his mouth upon the dust they lay)
And while there may be hope will not misdoubt.
His cheek to him that smiteth offers he,
And is content, though he reviled be.

11.

For sure is he (whatever doth befall)
The Lord will not forsake for evermore;
But that, he having punish'd, pity shall,
Because he many mercies hath in store.
For God in plaguing take no pleasure can,
Nor willingly afflicteth any man.

12.

The Lord delighteth not to trample down
Those men that here on earth enthralled are;

Or that a righteous man should be o'erthrown,
When he before the Highest doth appear.
Nor is the Lord well-pleased in the sight,
When he beholds the wrong subvert the right.

13.

Let no man mutter then, as if he thought
Some things were done in spite of God's decree;
For all things at his word to pass are brought,
That either for our good or evil be.
Why then lives man, such murmurs to begin?
Oh, let him rather murmur at his sin!

14.

Our own lewd courses let us search and try;
We may to thee again, O Lord, convert.
To God, that dwelleth in the heav'ns on high,
Let us (oh, let us) lift both hand and heart;
For we have sinned, we rebellious were,
And therefore was it that thou did'st not spare.

15.

For this (with wrath o'ershadow'd) thou hast chas'd,
And slaughter made of us, without remorse:
Thyself obscured with a cloud thou hast,
That so our prayers might have no recourse.
And lo, among the heathen people, we
As outcasts and off-scourings reckon'd be.

16.

Our adversaries all (and ev'ry where)
Themselves with open mouth against us set;
On us is fallen a terror and a snare,
Where ruin hath with desolation met:
And for the daughter of my people's cares,
Mine eyes doth cast forth rivulets of tears.

17.

Mine eyes perpetually were overflown,
And yet there is no ceasing of my tears;
For if the Lord in mercy look not down,
That from the heav'ns he may behold my cares,
They will not stint: but for my people's sake
Mine eyes will weep until my heart doth break.

18.

As when a bird is chased to and fro,
My foes pursued me, when cause was none;
Into the dungeon they my life did throw,
And there they rolled over me a stone.
The waters, likewise, overflow'd me quite,
And then, methought, I perished outright.

19.

Yet on thy name, oh Lord! I called there,
(E'en when in that low dungeon I did lie)

Whence thou wert pleased my complaint to hear,
Not slighting me, when I did sighing cry;
That very day I called, thou drew'st near,
And saidst unto me, that I should not fear.

20.

Thou, Lord, my soul maintainest in her right;
My life by thee alone redeemed was:
Thou hast, oh Lord! observed my despight :*
Vouchsafe thy judgment also in my cause:
For all the grudge they bear me thou hast seen,
And all their plots that have against me been.

21.

Thou heardst what slanders they against me laid,
And all those mischiefs that devis'd for me:
Thou notest what their lips of me have said,
E'en what their dayly closest whisperings be;
And how, whene'er they rise, or down do lie,
Their song and subject of their mirth am I.

22.

But, Lord, thou shalt reward and pay them all,
That meed their actions merit to receive;
Thy heavy malediction seize them shall;
E'en this, sad hearts, they shall for ever have;
And by thy wrath pursued they shall be driven.
Till they are chased out from under heaven.

* Wrongs.

LAMENT. IV.

S in the two first Elegies, the Prophet here begins by way of exclamation, and most passionately sets forth the cause of his complaining by a threefold explication: First, by expressing the dignity, sex, and age, of the persons miserably perishing in this calamity; as princes, priests, men, women, and children. Secondly, by paralleling their estate with that of brute creatures, and their punishment with Sodom's. Thirdly, by shewing the horrible effects which followed this calamity; as, the nobility being driven to clothe themselves from the dunghill, and women to feed on their own children, &c. After this he sheweth what are the causes of all that misery which he bewaileth. Secondly, declareth the vanity of relying on temporal consolations. Thirdly, setteth forth the power and fierceness of the Church's adversaries. Fourthly, prophesieth that even Christ was to suffer the fury of their malice, before God's wrath could be appeased. And lastly, assureth that the Church shall be at length delivered, and her enemies rewarded according to their wickedness. This Song may be sung to set before our eyes the severity of God's wrath against sin, to win us to repentance, and to comfort us upon our conversions.

SONG XXVII.

Sing this as the Fifth Song.

1.

HOW dim the gold doth now appear!
(That gold, which once so brightly shone:)
About the city, here and there,
the sanctuary-stones are thrown.
The sons of Sion, late compar'd
To gold (the richest in esteem)
Like potsheards are, without regard,
And base as earthen vessels seem.

2.

The monsters of the sea have care
The breasts unto their young to give;
But crueller my people are;
And, *Estridge-like, in deserts live.
With thirst the sucklings' tongues are dry,
And to their parched roofs they cleave:
For bread young children also cry,
But none at all they can receive.

3.

Those, that were us'd to dainty fare,
Now in the streets half-starved lie:

* Ostrich.

And they, that once did scarlet wear,
Now dunghill rags about them tie.
Yea, greater plagues my people's crime
Hath brought on them, than Sodom's were:
For that was sunk in little time,
And no prolonged death was there.

4.

Her Nazarites, whose whiteness was
More pure than either milk or snow,
Whose ruddiness did rubies pass,
Whose veins did like the sapphire show,
Now blacker than the coal are grown;
And in the streets unknown are they:
Their flesh is clung unto the bone,
And like a stick is dried away.

5.

Such, therefore, as the sword hath slain,
Are far in better case than those,
Who death for want of food sustain,
Whilst in the fruitful field it grows.
For when my people were distress'd.
E'en women (that should pity take)
With their own hands their children dress'd,
That so their hunger they might slake.

OF THE CHURCH.

6.

The Lord accomplish'd hath his wrath ;
His fierce displeasure forth is pour'd ;
A fire on Sion set he hath,
Which e'en her ground-work hath devour'd;
When there is neither earthly king,
Nor, through the whole world, one of all
Thoughts any foe to pass could bring,
That thus Jerusalem should fall.

7.

But this hath happened for the guilt
Of those that have her prophets been ;
And those, her wicked priests, that spilt
The blood of innocents therein.
Along the streets they stumbling went,
(The blindness of these men was such)
And so with blood they were besprent,*
That no man would their garments touch.

8.

Depart, depart ('twas therefore said)
From these pollutions get ye far ;
So, wand'ring to the heathen, fled,
And said there was no biding there.
And them the Lord hath now in wrath
Exil'd and made despised live ;

* Covered over, or polluted.

Yea, sent their priests and elders hath,
Where none doth honour to them give.

9.

And as for us, our eyes decay'd,
With watching vain reliefs, we have;
'Cause we expect a nation's aid,
That is unable us to save:
For at our heels so close they be,
We dare not in the streets appear;
Our end we, therefore, coming see,
And know our rooting-out is near.

10.

Our persecutors follow on,
As swift as eagles of the sky;
They o'er the mountains make us run,
And in the deserts for us lye:
Yea, they have Christ (our life) betray'd,
And caus'd him in their pits to fall:
(E'en him) beneath whose shade, we said,
We live among the heathen shall.

11.

O Edom! in the land of Huz
(Though yet o'er us triumph thou may)
Thou shalt receive this cup from us,
Be drunk, and hurl thy clothes away;

For when thy punishments for sins
Accomplished, oh Sion, be,
To visit Edom he begins,
And publick make her shame will he.

LAMENT. V.

N this Elegy the Prophet prayeth unto the Lord to remember and consider his people's afflictions, acknowledging before him their miseries, and presenting them unto him as distressed orphans, widows, and captives (by such humiliation) to win his compassion. He moveth him also, by repetition of the miserable ruin they were fallen into, by the noble possessions and dignities they had lost, by the base condition of those under whose tyranny they were brought, and by the generality of their calamity, from which no sex, age, nor degree escaped. Then (ingenuously confessing their sin to be the just cause of all this) glorifieth God, and concludeth this petitionary Ode with desiring that he would both give them grace to repent, and restore them to that peace which they formerly enjoyed. This elegiacal Song we may sing unto God in the behalf of many particular Churches, even in these times: especially if we

consider that mystical bondage, which the devil hath brought them into; and apply these complaints to those spiritual calamities, which are befallen them for their sins

SONG XXVIII.

Sing this as the Fifth Song.

1.

OH, mind thou, Lord, our sad distress;
   Behold, and think on our approach;
Our houses strangers do possess,
And on our heritage encroach.
Our mothers for their husbands grieve,
And of our fathers robb'd are we:
Yea, money we compell'd to give
For our own wood and water be.

2.

In persecution we remain,
Where endless labour try us doth;
And we to serve for bread are fain,
To Egypt and to Ashur both
Our fathers err'd, and, being gone,
The burden of their sin we bear:
E'en slaves the rule o'er us have won,
And none to set us free is, there.

3.

For bread our lives we hazard in
The perils which the deserts threat ;
And like an oven is our skin,
Both soil'd and parch'd for want of meat.
In Sion wives defiled were,
Deflowered were the virgins young,
(Through Judah's cities every where)
And princes by their hands were hung.

4.

Her elders disrespected* stood ;
Her young men they for grinding took ;
Her children fell beneath the wood,
And magistrates the gate forsook.
Their musick young men have forborne ;
Rejoicing in their hearts is none :
To mourning doth our dancing turn,
And from our head the crown is gone.

5.

Alas, that ever we did sin !
For therefore feels our heart these cares ;
For that our eyes have dimmed been,
And thus the hill of Sion fares.
Such desolation there is seen,
That now the foxes play thereon ;

*Original. "Were not honoured."

But thou for ever, Lord, hast been,
And without ending is thy throne.

6.

Oh, why are we forgotten thus?
So long time wherefore absent art?
Convert thyself, oh Lord, to us,
And we to thee shall soon convert.
Renew, oh Lord, those ages past,
In which thy favour we have seen!
For we extremely are debas'd,
And bitter hath thine anger been.

THE PRAYER OF DANIEL.

Dan. ix. 4.

THE Prophet Daniel, in this prayer, beseecheth God to be merciful unto his people in captivity; and these four things are principally considerable therein: First, an acknowledgment of God's power, justice, and mercy, with a confession that, from the highest to the lowest, they had broken his commandments, and were therefore justly punished. Secondly, it is

OF THE CHURCH.

confessed, that as their punishment is that which they deserved, so it is also the same that was foretold should come upon them. Thirdly, he beseecheth that God, for his own mercy's sake, and the sake of his Messias, would (nevertheless) be merciful unto them : as well in regard he had heretofore gotten glory by delivering them, as in respect they were his own elected people, and were already become a reproach unto their neighbours. This may be sung whensoever any of those judgments are poured out on the commonwealth, which the prophets have threatened for sin : or in our particular afflictions, we having first applied it by our meditations.

SONG XXIX.

Sing this as the Twenty-second Song.

1.

LORD God Almighty! great, and full of fear;
Who always art from breach of promise free,
And never failing to have mercy there,
Where they observe thy laws, and honour thee :
We have transgressed, and amiss have done ;
We disobedient and rebellious were ;
For from thy precepts we astray are gone,
And we departed from thy judgments are.

2.

We did thy servants' prophecies withstand,
Who to our dukes, our kings, and fathers came,
When they to all the people of the land
Proclaimed forth their message in thy name.
In thee, oh Lord! all righteousness appears,
But public shame to us doth appertain ;
E'en as with them of Judah now it fares,
And those that in Jerusalem remain.

3.

Yea, as to Israel now it doth befall,
Throughout those lands in which they scatter'd be;
For that their great transgression, wherewithal
They have transgressed, and offended thee.
To us, our kings, our dukes, and fathers, doth
Disgrace pertain (oh Lord) for angering thee :
Yet mercy, Lord our God, and pardon, both
To thee belong, though we rebellious be.

4.

We did (indeed) perversely disobey
Thy voice (oh Lord our God), and would not hear
To keep those laws thou didst before us lay,
By those thy servants, who thy prophets were.
E'en all that of the race of Israel be,
Against thy law have grievously misdone.

OF THE CHURCH.

And that they might not listen unto thee,
They backward from thy voice, oh Lord, are gone.

5.

On them, therefore, that curse and oath descended,
Which in the law of Moses written was;
(The servant of that God whom we offended,)
And now his speeches he hath brought to pass;
On us, and on our judges, he doth bring
  That plague, wherewith he threatened us and
    them;
For under heaven was never such a thing,
As now is fallen upon Jerusalem.

6.

As Moses' written law doth bear record,
Now all this mischief upon them is brought.
And yet we prayed not before the Lord,
That, leaving sin, we might his truth be taught:
For which respect, the Lord in wait hath laid,
That he on us inflict this mischief might:
And sith* his holy word we disobey'd,
In all his doings he remains upright.

7.

But now, oh Lord our God, who from the land
Of cruel Egypt brought thy people hast;

* Since.

And by the power of thy almighty hand,
Achiev'd a name, which to this day doth last;
Though we have sinned in committing ill,
Yet, Lord, by that pure righteousness in thee,
From thy Jerusalem, thy holy hill,
Oh let thy wrathful anger turned be!

8.

For through the gilt of our displeasing sin,
And for our fathers' faults, Jerusalem,
(Thy chosen people) hath despised been,
And are the scorn of all that neighbour them.
Now, therefore, to thy servant's prayer incline;
Hear thou his suit, oh God, and let thy face,
(E'en for the Lord's dear sake) vouchsafe to shine
Upon thy (now forsaken) holy place!

9.

Thine ears incline thou (oh, my God) and hear;
Lift up thine eyes, and us, oh, look upon;
Us, who forsaken with thy city are;
That city, where thy name is called on;
For we upon ourselves presume not thus
Before thy presence our request to make,
For aught that righteous can be found in us,
But for thy great and tender mercy's sake.

10.

Lord, hear (forgive, oh Lord) and weigh the same;
Oh, Lord, perform it, and no more defer,
For thine own sake, my God; for by thy name,
Thy city and thy people called are.

THE PRAYER OF JONAH.

Jonah ii.

JONAH, flying from God, and being preserved in a fish's belly, when he was cast into the sea, made this Prayer to praise God for delivering him in so great an extremity. And the principal things remarkable therein are these: First, the place where he prayed; Secondly, the terrible danger that enclosed him; Thirdly, the despair he was nigh falling into; Fourthly, God's mercy, with the Prophet's timely application thereof, and the comfort it infused into him: Fifthly, the occasions drawing men into such perils; Sixthly, the vow made upon his deliverance, and the reason of that vow. This burial of Jonas in the fishes' belly, and his deliverance from thence, was a type of the burial and resurrection of our blessed Saviour, Matth. xii., 4. This Prayer, therefore, we ought not only to sing historically to memorize this wondrous work of God, but to praise him also for the Resurrection of Christ, and raising mankind from that fearful and bottomless gulf of perdition, wherein it lay swallowed up, without possibility of redeeming itself.

SONG XXX.

Sing this as the Twenty-fourth Song.

1.

IN my distress to Thee I cried, oh Lord!
   And thou wert pleased my complaint to hear
Out from the bowels of the grave I roar'd,
And to my voice thou did'st incline thine ear;
For I amid the raging sea was cast,
And to the bottom there thou plung'd me hast.

2.

The floods did round about me circles make,
Thy waves and billows overflow'd me quite;
And then unto myself (alas) I said,
I am for evermore depriv'd thy sight:
Yet once again thou pleased art that I
Should to thy holy temple lift mine eyes.

3.

E'en to my soul the waters clos'd me had;
O'erswallow'd by the deeps, I fast was pent:
About my head the weeds a wreath had made;
Unto the mountains' bottoms down I went;
And so, that forth again I could not get,
The earth an everlasting bar has set.

4.

Then thou, oh Lord my God, then thou wert he,
That from corruption did'st my life defend:
For when my soul was like to faint in me,
Thou thither did'st into my thought descend.
And, Lord, my prayer thence to thee I sent,
Which upward to thy holy temple went.

5.

Those who believe in vain and foolish lies,
Despisers of their own good safety be;
But I will offer up the sacrifice
Of singing praises with my voice to thee:
And I will that perform, which vow'd I have,
For unto thee belongs it, Lord, to save.

THE PRAYER OF HABAKUK.

Habak. iii.

IN this petitionary and prophetical Hymn, the Deliverer of mankind is first prayed for. Secondly, the glorious majesty of his coming is described by excellent allegories, and by allusions to former deliverances vouchsafed to the Jews. Thirdly, here is foretold the overthrow of Antichrist, who shall be destroyed by the brightness of our Saviour's coming. Fourthly, here is set forth the state of the latter times. Fifthly, he expresseth the joy, confidence, and safety of the elect of God, even amid those terrors that shall await upon their Redeemer's coming. This Song is to be sung historically, in commemoration of the Church's deliverance by the first coming of Jesus Christ: and prophetically, to comfort us concerning that perfect delivery, assured at his second coming. For though the Prophet had some respect to the Jews' temporal deliverance, that he might comfort the Church in those times; yet the Holy Ghost had principal regard to the spiritual deliverance of his spiritual kingdom, the holy Catholic Church. And to her, and her enemies, do the names (of the Church's enemies), here mentioned, very properly agree. Nay, Cushan, signifying dark, black, or cloudy, and Midian, which is interpreted condemnation, or judgment, better suit unto the nature of those spiritual adversaries, whom they prefigured, than to those people who were literally so called. For none are so fitly termed People of Darkness, or of Condemnation, as the members of Antichrist, and the spiritual Babylon.

SONG XXXI.

1.

LORD, thy answer I did hear,
And I grew therewith afeard;
When the times at fullest are,
Let thy work be then declar'd:
When the time, Lord, full doth grow,
Then in anger mercy show.

2.

God 'mighty he came down;
Down he came from Theman-ward;
And the matchless Holy One,
From mount Paran forth appear'd,
Heav'n o'erspreading with his rays
And earth filling with his praise.

3.

Sun-like was his glorious light;
From his side there did appear
Beaming rays, that shined bright;
And his power he shrouded there.
Plagues before his face he sent;
At his feet hot coals there went.

4.

Where he stood he measure took
Of the earth, and view'd it well;
Nations vanish'd at his look;
Ancient hills to powder fell: *
Mountains old cast lower were,
For his ways eternal are.

5.

Cushan tents I saw diseas'd,†
And the Midian curtains quake.
Have the floods, Lord, thee displeas'd?
Did the floods thee angry make?
Was it else the sea that hath
Thus provoked thee to wrath?

6.

For thou rod'st thy horses there,
And thy saving chariots through:

* Original. "The Everlasting Mountains were scattered."
† Afflicted.

Thou didst make thy bow appear,
And thou didst perform thy vow:
Yea, thine oath and promise past
(To the tribes) fulfilled hast.

7.

Through the earth thou rifts didst make,
And the rivers there did flow:
Mountains, seeing thee, did shake,
And away the floods did go;
From the deep a voice was heard,
And his hands on high he rear'd.

8.

Both the sun and moon made stay,
And remov'd not in their spheres:
By thines arrows light went they,
By thy brightly shining spears.
Thou in wrath the land didst crush,
And in rage the nations thresh.

9.

For thy people's safe release,
With thy Christ, for aid went'st thou:
Thou hast also pierc'd the chief
Of the sinful household through:
And display'd them, till made bare
From the feet to neck they were.

10.

Thou, with javelins of their own,
Didst their armies leader strike:
For against me they came down,
To devour me, whirlwind-like;
And they joy in nothing more,
Than unseen to spoil the poor.

11.

Through the sea thou mad'st a way,
And didst ride thy horses there,
Where great heaps of water lay:
I the news thereof did hear,
And the voice my bowels shook:
Yea, my lips a quivering took.

12.

Rottenness my bones possest;
Trembling fear possessed me:
I that troublous day might rest:
For, when his approaches be
Onward to the people made,
His strong troops will them invade.

13.

Bloomless shall the fig-tree be,
And the vine no fruit shall yield;

OF THE CHURCH.

Fade shall then the olive-tree:
Meat shall none be in the field:
Neither in the fold or stall,
Flock or herd continue shall.

14.

Yet the Lord my joy shall be,
And in him I will delight;
In my God, that saveth me,
God the Lord, my only might:
Who my feet so guides, that I,
Hind-like, pace my places high.

THE HYMNS OF THE NEW TESTAMENT.

THESE five that next follow are the Hymns of the New Testament; between which, and the Songs of the Old Testament, there is great difference: for the Songs of the Old Testament were either thanksgivings for temporal benefits, typifying and signifying future benefits touching our redemption; or else Hymns prophetically foreshewing those mysteries which were to be accomplished at the coming of Christ. But these Evangelical Songs were composed, not for temporal but for spiritual things promised and figured by those temporal benefits mentioned in the Old Testament, and perfectly fulfilled in the New. Therefore, these Evangelical Hymns are more excellent than such as are merely prophetical; in regard the possession is to be preferred before the hope, and the end before the means of obtaining it.

MAGNIFICAT.

Luke i. 46.

THE blessed Virgin Mary, being saluted by the Angel Gabriel, and having by the Holy Ghost conceived our Redeemer Jesus Christ in her womb, was made fruitful also, in her soul, by the overshadowing of that Holy Spirit; and thereupon brought forth this evangelical and prophetical Hymn: wherein three things are principally observable. First, she praiseth God for his particular mercies and favour towards her. Secondly, she glorifies God for the general benefit of our redemption. Thirdly, she magnifies God for the particular grace vouchsafed unto the seed of Israel, according to what was promised to Abraham. This is the first Evangelical Song; and was indicted by the Holy Ghost, not only to be the Blessed Virgin's Thanksgiving, but to be sung by the whole Catholic Church (whom she typically personated) to praise God for our redemption and exaltation; and therefore it is worthily inserted into the Liturgy, that it may be perpetually and reverently sung.

SONG XXXII.

Sing this as the Third Song.

1.

THAT magnify'd the Lord may be,
　My soul now undertakes ;
And in the God that saveth me
　My Spirit merry makes.
For he vouchsafed hath to view
　His handmaid's poor degree ;
And lo, all ages that ensue,
　Shall blessed reckon me.

2.

Great things for me the Almighty does,
　And holy is his name ;
From age to age he mercy shows,
　On such as fear the same.
He by his arm declar'd his might,
　And this to pass hath brought,
That now the proud are put to flight,
　By what their hearts have thought.

3.

The mighty plucking from their seat,
　The poor he placed there ;

And for the hungry takes the meat
From such as wealthy are.
But, minding mercy, he hath show'd
His servant Isr'el grace,
As he to our forefathers vow'd,
To Abraham and his race.

BENEDICTUS.

LUKE i. 68.

ZACHARY the Priest, being (upon the birth of his son) inspired with the knowledge of our Redeemer's incarnation, sung the second Evangelical Hymn; in which two things are especially considerable:—First, he blesseth God, because, through the coming of Christ, all the promises made unto the Patriarchs and Prophets were fulfilled, for the salvation of his people. Secondly, he declareth the office and duty of his own Son, who was sent before to prepare the way of the Lord. This Song the Church hath worthily inserted into the Liturgy also, and we ought therefore to sing it reverently, in memorial of our Saviour's Incarnation; and to praise God both for the fulfilling of his promises, and for that means of our evangelical preparation which he vouchsafed, by sending his Forerunner.

SONG XXXIII.

Sing this as the Third Song.

1.

BLEST be the God of Israel,
   For he his people bought;
And in his servant David's house
   Hath great salvation wrought;
As by his Prophets he foretold,
   Since time began to be,
That from our foes we might be safe
   And from our haters free.

2.

That he might show our fathers grace,
   And bear in mind the same,
Which by an oath he vow'd unto
   Our father Abraham;
That from our adversaries freed,
   We serve him fearless might,
In righteousness and holiness,
   Our lifetime in his sight.

3.

And (of the Highest) thee, oh Child!
   The Prophet I declare,

Before the Lord his face to go,
   His coming to prepare ;
To teach his people how they shall
   That safety come to know,
Which, by remission of their sins,
   He doth on them bestow.

4.

For it is through the tender love
   Of God alone, whereby
That day-spring hath to visit us
   Descended from on high ;
To light them who in darkness sit,
   And in Death's shade abide,
And in the blessed way of peace
   Their wandering feet to guide.

THE SONG OF ANGELS.

Luke ii. 18.

THIS is the third Evangelical Song mentioned in the New Testament; and it was sung by a choir of Angels (at the birth of our blessed Saviour Jesus Christ), whose rejoicing shall be made complete by the redemption of mankind. In this Song they first glorify God, and then proclaim that happy peace and reconciliation, which his Son's Nativity should bring unto the world, rejoicing therein; and in that unspeakable goodwill and dear communion, which was thereby established between the godhead, the manhood, and them. We therefore ought to join with them in this Song, and sing it often, to praise God, and quicken faith and charity in ourselves.

SONG XXXIV.

THUS Angels sung, and thus sing we;
    To God on high all glory be;
Let him on earth his peace bestow,
And unto men his favour show,

NUNC DIMITTIS.

Luke ii. 29.

THE fourth Evangelical Hymn is this of Simeon, who, being in expectation of the coming of the Messias (which according to Daniel's seventy weeks, was in those days to be accomplished), it was revealed unto him, that he should not die till he had seen Christ: and, accordingly, he coming into the temple by the spirit's instigation (when he was presented there as the law commanded), both beheld and embraced his Redeemer. In this Song, therefore, he glorifieth God for the fulfilling of his promise made unto him; and joyfully confesseth Jesus Christ before all the people. In repeating this Hymn we ought also to confess our Redeemer: for Simeon was, as it were, the Church's speaker; and hath for us expressed that thankful joy, wherewithal we should be filled, when God enlightens us with the knowledge and spiritual vision of our Saviour.

SONG XXXV.

Sing this as the Third Song.

GRANT now in peace (that by thy leave)
    I may depart, oh Lord!
For thy salvation seen I have,
    According to thy word;
That which prepared was by thee,
    Before all people's sight,
Thy Israel's renown to be,
    And to the Gentiles light.

THE SONG OF MOSES AND THE LAMB.

REV. XV. 8.

THE fifth and last Song recorded in the New Testament is this, called by St. John, *The song of Moses and the Lamb*; being indeed the effect of that triumph Song, which the Saints and blessed Martyrs shall sing unto the honour of that Lamb of God, which taketh away the sins of the world, when they have gotten the victory over Antichrist. This Hymn the members of the true Church, may sing to God's glory, and the increase of their own comfort, when they perceive the power of the Almighty any way manifested upon that adversary. It may be repeated also amid our greatest persecutions, to strengthen our faith, and remember us, that whatsoever we suffer, there will come a day, wherein we shall have cause to make use of this Hymn with a perfect rejoicing.

SONG XXXVI.

Sing this as the Thirteenth Song.

1.

OH thou Lord, thou God of might,
 (Who dost all things work aright)
Whatsoe'er is done by thee,
Great and wondrous proves to be.

2.

True thy ways are, and direct,
Holy King of Saints elect,
And (oh, therefore) who is there,
That of thee retains no fear?

3.

Who is there that shall deny
Thy great Name to glorify?

For thou, Lord, and thou alone,
Art the perfect Holy One.

4.

In thy presence nations all
Shall to adoration fall;
For thy judgments now appear
Unto all men what they are.

Here end the Hymns of the New Testament.

THE TEN COMMANDMENTS.

Exod. xx.

ALTHOUGH the Decalogue be not originally in verse, yet among us it hath been heretofore usually sung; because, therefore, it may be a means to present these precepts somewhat the oftener to remembrance, make them the more frequently repeated, and stir up those who sing and hear them to the better performance of their duties, they are here also inserted and fitted to be sung.

SONG XXXVII.

Sing this as the Fourth Song.

THE Great Almighty spake, and thus said he:
I am the Lord thy God; and I alone
From cruel Egypt's thraldom set thee free:
And other Gods but me thou shalt have none.

 Have mercy, Lord, and so our hearts incline,
 That we may keep this blessed Law of thine.

Thou shalt not make an image, to adore,
Of aught on earth, above it, or below:
A carved work thou shalt not bow before;
Nor any worship on the same bestow.

For I, thy God, a jealous God am known,
And on their seed the fathers' sins correct,
Until the third and fourth descent be gone:
But them I always love, that me affect.

 Have mercy, Lord, and so our hearts incline,
 That we may keep this blessed Law of thine.

The Name of God thou never shalt abuse,
By swearing, or repeating it in vain:

For him that doth his Name profanely use,
The Lord will as a guilty-one arraign.
> *That we may keep this blessed Law of thine.*
> *Have mercy, Lord, and so our hearts incline,*

To keep the Sabbath holy, bear in mind;
Six days thine own affairs apply thou to;
The seventh is God's own day, for rest assign'd,
And thou no kind of work therein shalt do.

Thou, nor thy child, thy servants, nor thy beast;
Nor he that guest-wise with thee doth abide;
For after six days labour God did rest,
And therefore he that day hath sanctify'd.
> *Have mercy, Lord, and so our hearts incline,*
> *That we may keep this blessed Law of thine.*

See that unto thy parents thou do give
Such honour, as the child by duty owes;
That thou a long and blessed life may'st live,
Within the land the Lord thy God bestows.
> *Have mercy, Lord, and so our hearts incline,*
> *That we may keep this blessed Law of thine.*

Thou shalt be wary, that thou no man slay;
Thou shalt from all adultery be clear:
Thou shalt not steal another's goods away:
Nor witness false against thy neighbour bear.
> *Have mercy, Lord, and so our hearts incline*
> *That we may keep this blessed Law of thine.*

With what is thine remaining well apaid,
Thou shalt not covet what thy neighbour's is ;
His house nor wife, his servant, man nor maid,
His ox, nor ass, nor anything of his,
> *Thy mercy, Lord, thy mercy let us have,*
> *And in our hearts these Laws of thine engrave.*

THE LORD'S PRAYER.

MATT. vi. 7.

THE Lord's Prayer hath been anciently and usually sung also; and to that purpose was heretofore both translated and paraphrased in verse: which way of expression (howsoever some weak judgments have condemned it) doth no whit disparage or misbeseem a Prayer; for David made many prayers in verse: and, indeed, measured words were first devised and used to express the praises of God, and petitions made to him. Yea, those are the ancient and proper subjects of poesy, as appears throughout the sacred writ, and in the first human antiquities. Verse, therefore, dishonours not divine subjects; but those men do profane and dishonour verse, who abuse it on vain and mere profane expressions. The scope and use of this Prayer is so frequently treated of, that I think I shall not need to assist thereon in this place.

SONG XXXVIII.

Sing this as the Third Song.

OUR Father, which in Heaven art,
   We sanctify thy name:
Thy kingdom come: thy will be done
   In heaven and earth the same:
Give us this day our daily bread:
   And us forgive thou so,
As we on them that us offend
   Forgiveness do bestow:
Into Temptation lead us not,
   But us from evil free:
For thine the kingdom, power, and praise
   Is, and shall ever be.

THE APOSTLES CREED.

THE effect and use of this Creed is so generally taught, that this preface need not be enlarged: and as touching the singing and versifying of it, that which is said in the preface of the Lord's Prayer may serve for both.

SONG XXXIX.

1.

IN God the Father I believe,
  Who made all creatures by his word;
And true belief I likewise have
In Jesus Christ, his Son, our Lord;
Who by the Holy Ghost conceiv'd,
Was of the Virgin Mary born;
Who meekly Pilate's wrongs receiv'd,
And crucified was with scorn.

2.

Who died and in the grave hath lain,
Who did the lowest pit descend:

Who on the third day rose again,
And up to heaven did ascend.
Who at his father's right hand there
Now throned sits, and thence shall come
To take his seat of judgment here;
And give both quick and dead their doom.

3.

I in the Holy Ghost believe,
The holy Church Catholick too,
(And that the Saints communion have)
Undoubtedly believe I do.
I well assured am, likewise,
A pardon or my sins to gain;
And that my flesh from death shall rise,
And everlasting life obtain.

A FUNERAL SONG.

THE first stanza of this Song is taken out of St. John's Gospel, chap. xi. ver. 25, 26. The second stanza, Job xix. 25, 26, 27. The third stanza, 1 Tim., vi. 7, and Job i. 21. The last stanza, Rev. xiv., 13. And in the Order of Burial appointed by the Church of England, it [is appointed to be sung or read, as

OF THE CHURCH. 155

the minister pleaseth: that therefore it may be the more conveniently used either way, according to the Church's appointment, it is here turned into lyric verse. It was ordained to comfort the living, by putting them in mind of the Resurrection, and of the happiness of those who die in the faith of Christ Jesus.

SONG XL.

Sing this as the Ninth Song.

1.

I Am the Life (the Lord thus saith)
The Resurrection is through me;
And whosoe'er in me hath faith,
Shall live, yea, though now dead he be:
And he for ever shall not die,
That living doth on me rely.

2.

That my Redeemer lives, I ween,*
And that at last I rais'd shall be
From earth, and, cover'd with my skin
In this my flesh, my God shall see.
Yea, with these eyes, and these alone,
E'en I my God shall look upon.

* Know.

3.

Into the world we naked come,
And naked back again we go:
The Lord our wealth receive we from;
And he doth take it from us too:
The Lord both wills, and works the same,
And blessed therefore be his name.

4.

From Heaven there came a voice to me,
And this it will'd me to record;
The dead from henceforth blessed be,
The dead that dieth in the Lord:
The Spirit thus doth likewise say,
For from their works at rest are they.

THE SONG OF THE THREE CHILDREN.

THIS Song hath been anciently used in the Liturgy of the Church, as profitable to the stirring up of devotion, and for the praise of God: for it earnestly calleth upon all creatures to set forth the glory of their Creator, even angels, spirits, and reasonable creatures, with those also that are unreasonable, and unsensible. And this speaking to things without life is not to intimate that they are capable of such like exhortations; but rather, that upon consideration of the obedience which beasts and insensible creatures continue towards God, according to the law imposed at their creation, men might be provoked to remember the honour and praise, which they ought to ascribe unto their Almighty Creator, as well as all his other creatures.

SONG XLI.

Sing this as the Ninth Song.

1.

OH all you creatures of the Lord,
　　You Angels of the God most high;
You heavens, with what you do afford;
And waters all above the sky:

*Bless ye the Lord, him praise, adore,
And magnify him evermore.*

2.

Of God, you everlasting Powers,
Sun, moon, and stars, so bright that show;
You soaking dews, you dropping showers;
And all you winds of God that blow:

*Bless ye the Lord, him praise, adore,
And Magnify him evermore.*

3.

Thou fire, and what doth heat contain;
Cold winter, and thou summer fair;
You blustering storms of hail, and rain;
And thou, the frost-congealing air:

Bless ye the Lord, him praise, adore,
And Magnify him evermore.

4.

Oh praise him both, you ice and snow;
You nights and days, do you the same,
With what or dark or light doth show;
You clouds, and ev'ry shining flame.

Bless ye the Lord, him praise, adore,
And magnify him evermore.

5.

Thou earth, you mountains, and you hills,
And whatsoever thereon grows;
You fountains, rivers, springs, and rills;
You seas, and all that ebbs or flows;

Bless ye the Lord, him praise, adore,
And magnify him evermore.

6.

You whales, and all the water yields;
You of the feather'd airy breed;

You beasts and cattle of the fields;
And you that are of human seed:
> *Bless ye the Lord, him praise, adore,*
> *And magnify him evermore.*

7.

Let Israel the Lord confess;
So let his priests, that in him trust;
Him, let his servants also bless;
Yea, souls and spirits of the just:
> *Bless ye the Lord, him praise, adore,*
> *And magnify him evermore.*

8.

You blessed Saints, his praises tell;
And you that are of humble heart,
With Ananias, Misael;
And Azarias (bearing part):
> *Bless ye the Lord, him praise, adore,*
> *And magnify him evermore.*

THE SONG OF ST. AMBROSE;
OR TE DEUM.

THIS Song, commonly called *Te Deum*, or *the Song of St. Ambrose*, was repeated at the baptizing of St. Augustine; and (as it is recorded) was composed at that very time by those two reverend Fathers, answering one another, as it were by immediate inspiration. It is one of the most ancient Hymns of the Christian Church, excellently praising and confessing the blessed Trinity; and therefore is daily and worthily made use of in our Liturgy, and reckoned among the sacred Hymns.

SONG XLII.

Sing this as the Forty-fourth Song.

1.

WE praise thee, God, we acknowledge thee
    To be the Lord, for evermore:
And the eternal Father we,
Throughout the earth, do thee adore:

All Angels, with all powers within
The compass of the heavens high;
Both Cherubin, and Seraphin,
To thee perpetually do cry.

2.

Oh holy, holy, Holy One,
Thou Lord and God of Sabbath art;
Whose praise and majesty alone
Fills heaven and earth in ev'ry part:
The glorious troop apostolick,
The Prophets' worthy company;
The Martyrs' army royal eke*
Are those whom thou art praised by.

3.

Thou through the holy Church art known,
The Father of unbounded power:
Thy worthy, true, and only Son:
The Holy Ghost the Comforter:
Of glory, thou, oh Christ, art King;
The Father's Son, for evermore;
Who men from endless death to bring
The Virgin's womb didst not abhor.

4.

When Conqueror of Death thou wert,
Heaven to the faithful openedst thou;

* Also.

And in the Father's glory art
At God's right hand enthroned now:
Whence we believe that thou shalt come
To judge us in the day of wrath.
Oh, therefore, help thy servants, whom
Thy precious blood redeemed hath.

5.

Them with those saints do thou record,
That gain eternal glory may:
Thine heritage and people, Lord,
Save, bless, guide, and advance for aye.*
By us thou daily prais'd hast been,
And we will praise thee without end,
Oh keep us, Lord, this day from sin,
And let thy mercy us defend.

6.

Thy mercy, Lord, let us receive,
As we our trust repose in thee:
Oh, Lord, in thee I trusted have;
Confounded never let me be.

* Ever.

ATHANASIUS'S CREED;
OR, QUICUNQUE VULT.

THIS Creed was composed by Athanasius (after the wicked heresy of Arius had spread itself through the world,) that so the faith of the Catholic Church, concerning the mystery of the blessed Trinity, might be the better understood, and professed, to the overthrow and preventing of Arianism, or the like heresies. And to the same purpose it is appointed to be said or sung upon certain days of the year in the Church of England.

SONG XLIII.

Sing this as the Third Song.

1.

THOSE that will saved be, must hold
    The true Catholic Faith,
And keep it wholly, if they would
    Escape eternal death.
Which Faith a Trinity adores
    In One, and One in Three:

So, as the substance being one,
   Distinct the persons be.

2.

One Person of the Father is,
   Another of the Son,
Another of the Holy Ghost,
   And yet their godhead one:
Alike in glory; and in their
   Eternity as much;
For as the Father, both the Son
   And Holy Ghost is such.

3.

The Father uncreate, and so
   The Son and Spirit be:
The Father he is infinite;
   The other two as he.
The Father an eternal is,
   Eternal is the Son:
So is the Holy Ghost; yet these
   Eternally but One.

4.

Nor say we there are infinites,
   Or uncreated Three;
For there can but one infinite
   Or uncreated be.

OF THE CHURCH.

So Father, Son, and Holy Ghost
  All three Almighties are;
And yet not three Almighties though,
  But only One is there.

5.

The Father likewise God and Lord;
  And God and Lord the Son;
And God and Lord the Holy Ghost,
  Yet God and Lord but One.
For though each Person by himself
  We God and Lord confess,
Yet Christian faith forbids that we
  Three Gods or Lords profess.

6.

The Father not begot, nor made;
  Begot (not made) the Son;
Made, nor begot, the Holy Ghost,
  But a proceeding One.
One Father, not three Fathers, then;
  One only Son, not three;
One Holy Ghost we do confess,
  And that no more they be.

7.

And less, or greater than the rest,
  This Trinity hath none;

But they both co-eternal be,
   And equal ev'ry one.
He therefore that will saved be,
   (As we have said before)
Must One in Three, and Three in One,
   Believe, and still adore.

8.

That Jesus Christ incarnate was,
   He must believe with this;
And how that both the Son of God
   And God and Man he is.
God, of his Father's substance pure,
   Begot ere time was made:
Man of his mother's substance born,
   When time his fulness had.

9.

Both perfect God, and perfect Man,
   In soul, and flesh, as we;
The Father's equal being God
   As man beneath is he.
Though God and Man, yet but one Christ;
   And to dispose it so,
The Godhead was not turn'd to flesh,
   But manhood took thereto.

10.

The substance unconfus'd; he one
    In person doth subsist:
As soul and body make one man,
    So God and Man is Christ;
Who suffer'd, and went down to hell,
    That we might saved be';
The third day he arose again,
    And Heaven ascended he.

11.

At God the Father's right hand there
    He sits; and at the doom,
He to adjudge both quick and dead,
    From thence again shall come.
Then all men with their flesh shall rise,
    And he account require:
Well-doers into bliss shall go,
    The bad to endless fire.

VENI CREATOR.

THIS is a very ancient Hymn, composed in Latin rhyme, and commonly called *Veni Creator*, because those are the first words of it. By the canons of our Church it is commanded to be said or sung at the consecration of Bishops, and at the ordination of Ministers, etc. It is therefore here translated syllable for syllable, and in the same kind of measure which it hath in the Latin.

SONG XLIV.

1.

COME Holy Ghost, the Maker, come;
Take in the souls of thine thy place;
Thou whom our hearts had being from,
Oh, fill them with thy heavenly grace.
Thou art that Comfort from above,
The Highest doth by gift impart;
Thou spring of life, a fire of love,
And the anointing Spirit art.

OF THE CHURCH.

2.

Thou in thy gifts art manifold;
God's right-hand finger thou art, Lord:
The Father's promise made of old;
Our tongues enriching by thy word.
Oh! give our blinded senses light:
Shed love into each heart of our,
And grant the body's feeble plight
May be enabled by thy power.

3.

Far from us drive away the foe,
And let a speedy peace ensue:
Our leader also be, that so
We every danger may eschew.
Let us be taught the blessed Creed
Of Father, and of Son, by thee:
And how from both thou dost proceed,
That our belief it still may be.

To thee, the Father, and the Son,
(Whom past and present times adore)
The One in Three, and Three in One,
All glory be for evermore!

**HERE ENDS THE FIRST PART OF THE HYMNS
AND SONGS OF THE CHURCH.**

THE SECOND PART
OF THE HYMNS AND SONGS OF THE CHURCH.

EVERY thing hath his season, saith the Preacher, Eccl. iii. And St. Paul adviseth, 'That all things should be done honestly, in order, and to edification,' 1 Cor. xiv. Which council the Church religiously heeding (and how, by observation of times, and other circumstances, the memories and capacities of weak people were the better assisted) it was provided, that there should be annual commemorations of the principal mysteries of our redemption: and certain particular days were dedicated to that purpose, as nigh as might be guessed (for the most part) upon those very seasons of the year, in which the several mysteries were accomplished. And, indeed, this is not that heathenish or idolatrous heeding of times, reprehended in Isaiah xlvii.; nor such a Jewish or superstitious observation of days, and months, and times, and years, as is reproved by St. Paul, Gal. iv. Nor a toleration for idleness, contrary to the fourth commandment; but a Christian and warrantable observation, profitably ordained, that things might be done in order, that the understanding might be the better edified; that the memory might be the oftener refreshed; and that the devotion might be the more stirred up.

It is true, that we ought to watch every hour: but if the Church had not by her authority appointed set days and hours to keep us awake in, some of us would hardly watch one hour: and therefore, those who have zeal according to knowledge, do not only religiously observe the Church's appointed times, but do, by her example, voluntarily also appoint unto themselves certain days, and hours of the day, for Christian exercises. Neither can any man suppose this commendable observation of feasts (neither burdensome by multitude, nor superstitious by institution) to be an abridgment of Christian liberty, who, as he ought to do, believeth that the service of God is perfect freedom. We persuade not, that one day is more holy than another in his own nature; but admonish that those be reverently and christianly observed, which are, upon so good ground, and with prudent moderation, dedicated to the worship of God: for, it cannot be denied, that even those who are but coldly affected to the Church's ordinances in this kind, do nevertheless often apprehend the mystery of Christ's Nativity and Passion, upon the days of commemorating them, much more feelingly than at other times: and that they forget also some other mysteries altogether, until they are remembered of them by the distinction and observation of times used in the Church.

These things considered; and because there be many, who, through ignorance rather than obstinacy, have neglected the Church's ordinance in this point, here are added (to those Songs of the Church which were either taken out of the canonical Scripture, or anciently in use) certain other Spiritual Songs and Hymns, appropriated to those days and occasions which are most observable throughout the year. And before each several Hymn is prefixed a brief Preface also, to declare their use, and the purpose of each commemoration; that such, who have heretofore through ignorance contemned the Church's discipline therein, might behave themselves more reverently hereafter, and learn not to speak evil of those things they understand not.

ADVENT SUNDAY.

THE Advent is that for Christmas, which John Baptist was to Christ (even a forerunner for preparation): and it is called the Advent (which signifieth coming) because the Church did usually, from that time until the Nativity, commemorate the several comings of Christ, and instruct the people concerning them. Which comings are these, and the like: His Conception, by which he came into the Virgin's womb: His Nativity, by which he came (as it were) further into the world: His coming to preach in his own person: His coming by his Ministers: His coming to Jerusalem: The coming of the Holy Ghost: His spiritual coming, which he vouchsafeth into the heart of every regenerate Christian: And finally, that last coming of his, which shall be unto judgment, &c. All which comings are comprehended in these three; his coming to men, into men, and against men; to men, by his Incarnation; into men, by Grace; against men, to Judgment.

SONG XLV.

Sing this as the Ninth Song.

1.

WHEN Jesus Christ incarnate was,
    To be our brother then came he:
When into us he comes by grace,
Then his beloved spouse are we:
When he from Heaven descends again,
To be our judge returns he then.

2.

And then despair will those confound,
That his first comings nought regard;
And those, who till the trumpet sound,
Consume their leisures unprepar'd:
Curst be those pleasures, cry they may,
Which drove the thought of this away.

3.

The Jews abjected yet remain,
That his first advent heeded not;
And those five virgins knock'd in vain,
Who to provide them oil forgot:
But safe and blessed those men are,
Who for his comings do prepare.

4.

O let us therefore watch and pray,
His times of visiting to know;
And live so furnish'd, that we may
With him unto his wedding go:
Yea, though at midnight he should call,
Let us be ready, lamps, and all.

5.

And so provide before that feast,
Which Christ his coming next doth mind,
That he to come, and be a guest
Within our hearts, may pleasure find;
And we bid welcome, with good cheer,
That coming, which so many fear.

6.

Oh come, Lord Jesu, come away;
(Yea, though the world it shall deter)
Oh let thy kingdom come, we pray,
Whose coming most too much defer:
And grant us thereof such foresight,
It come not like a thief by night.

CHRISTMAS DAY.

THIS day is worthily dedicated to be observed in remembrance of the blessed Nativity of our Redeemer Jesus Christ: at which time it pleased the Almighty Father to send his only begotten Son into the world for our sakes; and by an unspeakable union to join in one person God and Man, without confusion of natures, or possibility of separation. To express, therefore, our thankfulness, and the joy we ought to have in this love of God, there hath been anciently, and is yet continued in England (above other countries), a neighbourly and plentiful hospitality in inviting, and (without invitation) receiving unto our wellfurnished tables, our tenants, neighbours, friends, and strangers; to the honour of our nation, and increase of amity and free-hearted kindness among us. But, most of all, to the refreshing of the bowels of the poor, being the most Christian use of such festivals. Which charitable and good English custom hath of late been seasonably re-advanced by his Majesty's gracious care, in commanding our Nobility and Gentry to repair (especially at such times) to their country mansions

SONG XLVI.

1.

AS on the night before this blessed morn
  A troop of Angels unto Shepherds told,
Where in a stable he was poorly born,
Whom nor the earth nor heaven of heavens can hold,
  Through Bethlehem rung,
  This news at their return;
  Yea, Angels sung,
  That GOD WITH US was born:
And they made mirth, because we should not mourn.

CHORUS.

Their Angels caroll sing we then,
To God on high all glory be;
For peace on earth bestoweth he,
And sheweth favour unto men.

2.

This favour Christ vouchsafeth for our sake:
To buy us thrones he in a manger lay;
Our weakness took, that we his strength might take,
And was disrob'd, that he might us array,
  Our flesh he wore,
  Our sin to wear away:
  Our curse he bore,
  That we escape it may;
And wept for us, that we might sing for aye.*

With Angels therefore sing again,
To God on high all glory be;
For peace on earth bestoweth he,
And sheweth favour unto men

* Ever.

SONG XLVII.

ANOTHER FOR CHRISTMAS-DAY.

1.

A SONG of Joy unto the Lord we sing,
And publish forth the favours he hath shown:
We sing his praise, from whom all joy doth spring,
And tell abroad the wonders he hath done;
For such were never since the world begun.
> *His love, therefore, oh ! let us all confess*
> *And to the sons of men his works express.*

2.

As on this day the Son of God was born,
The blessed Word was then incarnate made;
The Lord to be a servant held no scorn:
The Godhead was with human nature clad,
And flesh a throne above all Angels had.
> *His love therefore, &c.*

3.

Our sin and sorrows on himself he took,
On us his bliss and goodness to bestow:
To visit earth, he Heaven awhile forsook;
And to advance us high, descended low;
But with the sinful angels dealt not so.
> *His love therefore, &c.*

4.

A maid conceiv'd, whom man had never known :
The fleece was moistened, where no rain had been :
A virgin she remains that had a son :
The bush did flame that still remained green ;
And this befell, when God with us was seen.
His love therefore, &c.

5.

For sinful men all this to pass was brought,
As, long before, the Prophets had forespoke ;
So he, that first our shame and ruin wrought,
Once bruis'd our heel, but now his head is broke :
And he hath made us whole, who gave that stroke.
His love therefore, &c.

6.

The Lamb hath played devouring wolves among;
The morning star of Jacob doth appear ;
From Jesse's root our tree of life is sprung,
And all God's works (in him) fufilled are :
Yet we are slack his praises to declare.
His love therefore, &c.

THE CIRCUMCISION,

OR NEW YEAR'S DAY.

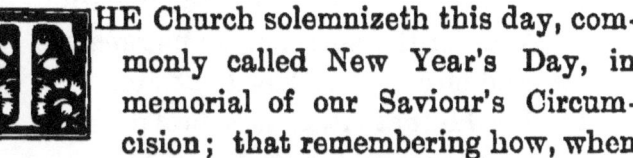THE Church solemnizeth this day, commonly called New Year's Day, in memorial of our Saviour's Circumcision; that remembering how, when he was but eight days old, he began to smart and shed his blood for us, we might praise him for the same; and that with due thankfulness, considering how easy a sacrament he hath left us (instead of that bloody one, which the law enjoined) we might be provoked to bring forth the fruits of regeneration.

SONG XLVIII.

Sing this as the Forty-fourth Song.

1.

THIS day thy flesh, oh Christ, did bleed,
    Mark'd by the circumcision-knife:
Because the law, for man's misdeed,
Requir'd that earnest of thy life:]
Those drops divin'd that shower of blood,
Which in thine agony began:

And that great shower foreshew'd the flood
Which from thy side the next day ran.

2.

Then, through that milder sacrament
Succeeding this, thy grace inspire;
Yea, let thy smart make us repent,
And circumcised hearts desire,
For he that either is baptiz'd,
Or circumcis'd in flesh alone,
Is but as an uncircumcis'd,
Or as an unbaptized one.

3.

The year anew we now begin,
And outward gifts receiv'd have we;
Renew us also, Lord, within,
And make us new year's gifts for thee
Yea, let us, with the passed year,
Our old affections cast away;
That we new creatures may appear,
And to redeem the time essay.

TWELFTH-DAY,

OR THE EPIPHANY.

TWELFTH-DAY, otherwise called the Epiphany, or the Day of Manifestation, is celebrated by the Church to the praise of God, and in memorial of that blessed and admirable discovery of our Saviour's birth, which was vouchsafed unto the Gentiles shortly after it came to pass. For as the Shepherds of the Jews were warned thereof, and directed to the place by an Angel from Heaven; so the Magi of the Gentiles received the same particular notice of it by a star in the East, that both Jews and Gentiles might be left inexcusable, if they came not to his worship. This day is observed also in commemoration of our Saviour's Baptism, and of his first miracle in Canaan, by which he was likewise manifested to be the Son of God.

SONG XLIX.

Sing this as the Forty-first Song.

1.

THAT so thy blessed birth, oh Christ,
    Might through the world be spread about,
Thy star appeared in the East,
Whereby the Gentiles found thee out:
And offering thee myrrh, incense, gold,
Thy three-fold office did unfold.

2.

Sweet Jesus let that star of thine,
Thy grace, which guides to find out thee,
Within our hearts for ever shine,
That thou of us found out may'st be:
And thou shalt be our King, therefore,
Our Priest and Prophet evermore.

3.

Tears that from true repentance drop,
Instead of myrrh, present will we:
For incense we will offer up
Our prayers and praises unto thee;
And bring for gold each pious deed,
Which doth from saving grace proceed.

4.

And as those Wise Men never went
To visit Herod any more;
So, finding thee, we will repent
Our courses follow'd heretofore:
And that we homeward may retire,
The way by thee we will inquire.

THE PURIFICATION OF ST.
MARY THE VIRGIN.

ACCORDING to the time appointed to in the law of Moses, the blessed Virgin St. Mary reckoned the days of Purification, which were to be observed after the birth of a male child: and then, as the law commanded, presented both her son and her appointed offering in the Temple. Partly, therefore, in commemoration of that her true obedience to the law, and partly to memorize that presentation of our Redeemer (which was performed by his blessed mother at her Purification) this anniversary is worthily observed.

SONG L.

Sing this as the Ninth Song.

1.

NO doubt but she that had the grace,
    Thee in her womb, oh Christ, to bear,
And did all womankind surpass,
Was hallow'd by thy being there;
And where the fruit so holy was,
The birth could no pollution cause.

2.

Yet in obedience to thy law,
Her purifying rites were done,
That we might learn to stand in awe,
How from thine ordinance we run;
For if we disobedient be,
Unpurified souls have we.

3.

Oh keep us, Lord, from thinking vain,
What by thy word thou shalt command:
Let us be sparing to complain,
On what we do not understand;
And guide thy Church, that she may still
Command, according to thy will.

4.

Vouchsafe that with one joint consent
We may thy praises ever sing;
Preserve thy seamless robe unrent,
For which so many lots do fling:
And grant that, being purified
From sin, we may in love abide,

5.

Moreover, as thy mother went
(That holy and thrice blessed maid)
Thee in thy Temple to present,
With perfect human flesh array'd;
So let us, offer'd up to thee,
Replenish'd with thy Spirit be.

6.

Yea, let thy Church, our mother dear,
(Within whose womb new-born we be)
Before thee at her time appear,
To give her children up to thee;
And take, for purified things,
Her, and that offering which she brings.

THE FIRST DAY OF LENT.

THE observation of Lent is a profitable institution of the Church, not abridging the Christian liberty of meats, but intended for a means to help to set the spirit at liberty from the flesh: and therefore this fast consisteth not altogether in a formal forbearance of this or that food, but in a true mortification of the body: for abstinence from flesh only (wherein also we ought to be obedient to the higher powers) more tendeth to the increase of plenty and well-ordering things in the common-wealth, than to a spiritual discipline. Because it is apparent we may over-pamper ourselves, as well with what is permitted as with what is forbidden; this commendable observation (which every man ought to observe so far forth as he shall be able, and his spiritual necessity requires) was appointed; partly to commemorate our Saviour's miraculous fasting, whereby he satisfied for the gluttony of our first parents; and (at this season) partly to cool our wanton blood, which at this time of the year is aptest to be enflamed with evil concupiscences; and partly, also, to prepare us the better both to meditate the passion of our Saviour, which is always commemorated about the end of Lent, and to fit us to receive the blessed Sacrament of his Last Supper to our greater comfort.

SONG LI.

Sing this as the Forty-fourth Song.

1.

THY wondrous fasting to record,
  And our rebellious flesh to tame,
A holy fast to thee, oh Lord,
We have intended in thy name:
Oh sanctify it, we thee pray,
That we may thereby honour thee;
And so dispose us, that it may
To our advantage also be.

2.

Let us not grudgingly abstain
Nor secretly the gluttons play,
Nor openly, for glory vain,
Thy Church's ordinance obey;
But let us fast, as thou has taught,
Thy rule observing in each part,
With such intentions as we ought,
And with true singleness of heart.

3.

So thou shalt our devotions bless
And make this holy discipline

A means that longing to suppress,
Which keeps our will so cross to thine:
And though our strictest fastings fail
To purchase of themselves thy grace,
Yet they do make for our avail
(By thy deservings) shall have place.

4.

True fasting helpful oft have been,
The wanton flesh to mortify;
But takes not off the guilt of sin,
Nor can we merit ought thereby:
It is thine abstinence, or none,
Which merit favour for us must;
For when our glorioust works are done,
We perish, if in them we trust.

THE ANNUNCIATION OF MARY.

THE Church hath dedicated this day to memorize the Annunciation of the blessed Virgin St. Mary, who was about this time of the year saluted by the Angel Gabriel; and we ought to sanctify it with praising God for that inexpressible mystery of our Saviour's conception, which was the happy news the holy Angel brought unto his mother. Nothing in the world is more worthy to be spoken of than this favour, and yet nothing more unspeakable.

SONG LII.

Sing this as the Forty-fourth Song.

1.

OUR hearts, O blessed God incline,
　　Thy true affection to embrace ;
And that humility of thine,
Which for our sakes vouchsafed was,
Thy goodness teach us to put on,
As with our nature thou wert clad ;
And so to mind what thou hast done,
That we may praise thee, and be glad.

2.

For thou not only held'st it meet
To send an angel from above,
An humble maid on earth to greet,
And bring the message of thy love ;
But laying (as it were) aside
Those glories none can comprehend,
Nor any mortal eyes abide,
Into her womb thou didst descend.

8.

Bestow thou also thy respect
On our despised and low degree;
And, Lord, oh, do not us neglect,
Though worthy of contempt we be:
But through thy messengers prepare
And hallow so our hearts we pray,
That thou conceived being there
The fruits of faith bring forth we may.

PALM SUNDAY.

PALM Sunday is so called, by reason it was upon that day in which Jesus riding to Jerusalem (according to the Prophets), the people strewed the way for him with their garments, and the branches of the Palm Tree. And, indeed, it was in a manner the day of proclaiming him King, as the Friday following was the day of his coronation. Worthily, therefore, is it commemorated: and many excellent mysteries are thereby brought to remembrance, which, but for this anniversary, most would forget, and many perhaps never come to know.

SONG LIII.

Sing this as the Third Song.

1.

WHEN Jesus to Jerusalem,
    (And there to suffer) rode,
The people al the way for him
With palm and garments strow'd:
And though he did full meekly ride,
And poorly on an ass,
"Hosanna to the King!" they cried,
As he along did pass.

2.

His glory, and his royal right,
(E'en by a power divine)
As if, in wordly pomp's despite,
Through poverty did shine;
And though the greater sort did frown,
He exercis'd his power,
Till he himself did lay it down,
At his appointed hour.

8.

Possession of his house he got,
The merchants thence expell'd;

And though the priests were mad thereat,
His lectures there he held.
Oh! how should any be so dull,
To doubt who this might be?
When they did things so wonderful
And works so mighty, see.

4.

Lord, when to us thou drawest nigh,
Instruct us thee to know;
And to receive thee joyfully,
How mean so ere in show;
Yea, though the rich and worldly-wise,
When we thy praises sing,
Both thee, and us, therefore despise,
Be thou approv'd our King.

THURSDAY BEFORE EASTER.

AS upon this day our blessed Saviour eating the Passover with his disciples, instituted the blessed Sacrament of his Last Supper; afterwards he washed their feet; prayed for them, and for all the faithful generation; instructed them; comforted them; warned them of what should come to pass, both concerning them-

OF THE CHURCH. 195

selves, and his own death and resurrection; promised to send them a Comforter; and expressed many other excellent things for the confirmation of their faith. Then departing to a garden, he praying, fell into his most bitter agony, which having overcome, he was that night betrayed, and forsaken of all his disciples. In commemoration of which passages, the Church holds this yearly assembly, that our pious affections towards our Redeemer may be stirred up, to his glory, and our comfort.

SONG LIV.

Sing this as the Ninth Song.

1.

A HOLY Sacrament this day,
To us thou didst, oh Lord, bequeath;
That by the same preserve we may
A blest memorial of thy death;
Whereof, oh, let us so partake,
We may with thee one body make.

2.

Thy Holy Supper being done,
The last which thou vouchsafed'st here,
By thee the feet of every one
Of thy disciples washed were;

To which humility of thine,
Our haughty minds do thou incline.

3.

The rest of that day thou didst use,
To pray, to comfort, and advise:
None might, when thou wert gone, abuse
Thy friends, or make of them a prize;
Yet when thy pleasure thou hadst said,
By one of thine thou wert betray'd.

4.

And lo, that night they all did fly,
Who sate so kindly by thy side;
E'en he, that for thy love would die,
With oaths, and curses, thee deny'd;
Which to thy soul more nigh did go,
Than all the wrongs thy foes could do.

5.

Sweet Jesus, teach us to conceive,
How near unto thy heart it strook,*
When thy beloved thee did leave,
And thou didst back upon him look:
We may hereafter nigh thee keep,
And for our past denials weep.

* Struck.

OF THE CHURCH.

6.

Yea, let each passage of this day
Within our hearts be graven so,
That mind them we for ever may,
And still thy promise trust unto :|
So our affections shall to thee,
In life and death, unchanged be.

FRIDAY BEFORE EASTER.

THIS day we commemorate the insufferable passion of Jesus Christ, our blessed Redeemer; who was at this season of the year despitefully crucified by Pilate and the Jews. Every day we ought seriously to think upon it by ourselves; but this day we ought to meet about it in the public assemblies, that we might provoke each other to compunction of heart; to renew the memory of it; and to move those that have not yet taken notice thereof, to come along with us to hear the story of his unmatchless sorrow, who for the love of us took upon himself those punishments which our wickedness deserved.

SONG LV.

Sing this as the Twenty-fourth Song.

1.

YOU that like heedless strangers pass along,
 As if nought here concerned you to day;
Draw nigh and hear the saddest passion song,
That ever you did meet with in your way:
So sad a story ne'er was told before,
Nor shall there be the like for evermore.

2.

The greatest King that ever wore a crown,
More than the basest vassal was abus'd;
The truest lover that was ever known,
By them he lov'd was most unkindly us'd:
And he that liv'd from all transgressions clear,
Was plagu'd for all the sins that ever were.

3.

E'en they, in pity of whose fall he wept,
Wrought for his ruin, while he sought their good;
And watched for him, when they should have slept,
That they might quench their malice in his blood:
Yet (when their bonds from him he could have thrown),
To save their lives he deign'd to lose his own.

4.

Those, in whose hearts compassion should have
   been,
Insulted o'er his poor afflicted soul;
And those that nothing ill in him had seen,
(As guilty), him accus'd of treason foul :
Nay, him (that never had one idle thought),
They for blaspheming unto judgment brought.

5.

Where, some to ask him vain demands begin ;
And some to make a sport with him devise :
Some at his answers and behaviour grin,
And some do spit their filth into his eyes :
Some give him blows, some mock, and some revile,
And he (good heart), sits quiet all the while.

6.

Oh that, where such a throng of men should be,
No heart was found, so gentle to relent !
And that so good and meek a Lamb as he
Should be so us'd, and yet no tear be spent !
Sure, when once malice fills the heart of man,
Nor stone, nor steel, can be so hardened then.

7.

For, after this, his clothes from him they stript,
And then, as if some slave this Lord had been,

With cruel rods and scourges him they whipt,
Till wounds were over all his body seen :
In purple clad, and crowned too with thorn,
They set him forth, and honour'd him in scorn.

8.

And, when they saw him in so sad a plight,
As might have made a flinty heart to bleed,
They not a whit recanted at the sight,
But in their hellish fury did proceed :
Away with him! Away with him! they said ;
And, Crucify him! Crucify him! cried.

9.

A cross of wood, that huge and heavy was,
Upon his bloody shoulders next they lay ;
Which onward to his execution place
He carried, till he fainted in the way :
And when he thither weak and tired came,
To give him rest, they nail'd him to the same.

10.

Oh! could we but the thousandth part relate,
Of those afflictions, which they made him bear ;
Our hearts with passion would dissolve thereat,
And we should sit and weep for ever here :
Nor should we glad again hereafter be,
But that we hope in glory him to see.

11.

For while upon the cross he pained hung,
And was with soul-tormentings also griev'd,
(Far more than can be told by any tongue,
Or in the hearts of mortals be conceiv'd)
Those, for whose sake he underwent such pain,
Rejoic'd thereat, and held him in disdain.

12.

One offer'd to him vinegar and gall;
A second did his pious works deride;
To dicing for his robes did others fall;
And many mock'd him, when to God he cried;
Yet he, as they his pain still more procur'd,
Still lov'd, and for their good the more endur'd.

13.

But, though his matchless love immortal were,
It was a mortal body he had on,
That could no more than mortal bodies bear;
Their malice, therefore, did prevail thereon:
And lo, their utmost fury having tried,
This Lamb of God gave up the Ghost, and died.

14.

Whose death, though cruel unrelenting man
Could view, without bewailing, or affright

The sun grew dark, the earth to quake began,
The Temple veil did rend asunder quite ;
Yea, hardest rocks therewith in pieces brake,
And graves did open, and the dead awake.

15.

Oh, therefore, let us all that present be,
This innocent with moved souls embrace ;
For this was our Redeemer, this was he,
Who thus for our unkindness used was :
E'en he, the cursed Jews and Pilate slew,
Is he alone, of whom all this is true.

16.

Our sins of spite were part of those that day,
Whose cruel whips and thorns did make him smart;
Our lusts were those that tir'd him in the way ;
Our want of love was that which pierc'd his heart :
And still when we forget, or slight his pain,
We crucify and torture him again.

EASTER DAY.

THIS day is solemnised in memorial of our Saviour's blessed Resurrection from the dead; upon which (as the members with their head) the Church began her triumph over sin, death, and the devil; and hath, therefore appointed, that to record this mystery, and to stir up thankful rejoicings in our hearts, there should be an annual commemoration thereof: that we might, in charitable feasts and Christian glee, express the joy of our hearts to the glory of God, to the comfort of our brethren, to the increase of charity one towards another, and to the confirmation of a true joy in ourselves.

SONG LVI.

Sing this as the Forty-fourth Song.

1.

THIS is the day the Lord hath made,
And therein joyful we will be:
For from the black infernal shade
In triumph back returned is he:

The snares of Satan and of Death,
He hath victoriously undone,
And fast in chains he bound them hath,
His triumph to attend upon.

2.

The grave, which all men did detest,
And held a dungeon full of fear.
Is now become a bed of rest,
And no such terrors find we there,
For Jesus Christ hath took away
The horror of that loathed pit;
E'en ever since that glorious day,
In which himself came out of it.

3.

His mockings, and his bitter smarts,
He to our praise and ease doth turn,
And all things to our joy converts,
Which he with heavy heart hath borne:
His broken flesh is now our food,
His blood he shed, is ever since
That drink, which doth our souls most good,
And that which shall our foulness cleanse.

4.

Those wounds so deep, and torn so wide,
As in a rock our shelters are;

That, which they pierced through his side,
Is made a dove-hole for his dear;
Yea, now we know, as was foretold,
His flesh did no corruption see;
And that hell wanted strength to hold
So strong, and one so blest as he.

5.

O let us praise his name therefore,
(Who thus the upper hand hath won)
For we had else, for evermore,
Been lost, and utterly undone:
Whereas this favour doth allow
That we with boldness thus may sing,
Oh Hell, where is thy conquest now?
And thou (oh Death), where is thy sting

ASCENSION DAY.

AFTER Jesus Christ was risen from the dead, and had many times shewed himself unto his disciples, he was lifted from among them, and they beheld him ascending up into Heaven, till a cloud took him out of their sight. In memory of which Ascension, and to praise God for so exalting the human nature to his own glory, and our advantage, the Church worthily celebrated this day, and hath commended the observation thereof to her children.

SONG LVII.

Sing this as the Third Song.

1.

TO God, with heart and cheerful voice,
    A Triumph Song we sing;
And with true thankful hearts rejoice
In our Almighty King;
Yea, to his glory we record,
(Who were but dust and clay)
What honour he did us afford
On his ascending day.

2.

The human nature, which of late,
Beneath the angels was,
Now raised from that meaner state,
Above them hath a place.
And at man's feet all creatures bow,
Which through the whole world be,
For at God's right-hand throned now,
In glory sitteth he.

3.

Our Lord, and Brother, who hath on
Such flesh, as this we wear,
Before us unto Heaven is gone,
To get us places there:
Captivity was captiv'd then,
And he doth from above
Send ghostly presents down to men,
For tokens of his love.

4.

Each door and everlasting gate
To him hath lifted been;
And in a glorious wise thereat
Our King is enter'd in.
Whom if to follow we regard,
With ease we safely may,
For he hath all the means prepar'd,
And made an open way.

5.

Then follow, follow on a pace,
And let us not forego
Our Captain, till we win the place,
That he hath scaled unto:
And for his honour, let our voice
A shout so hearty make,
The Heavens may at our mirth rejoice,
And Earth and Hell may shake.

PENTECOST, OR WHITSUNDAY.

AFTER our Saviour was ascended, the fiftieth day of his Resurrection, and just at the Jews' Feast of Pentecost, the Holy Ghost (our promised Comforter) was sent down upon the Disciples assembled in Jerusalem, appearing in a visible form, and miraculously filling them with all manner of spiritual gifts and knowledge, tending to the divine work they had in hand; whereby, they being formerly weak and simple men, were immediately enabled to resist all the powers of the kingdom of darkness, and to lay those strong foundations, upon which the Catholic Church now standeth, both to the glory of God, and our safety. In remembrance, therefore, of that great miraculous mystery, this day is solemnized.

SONG LVIII.

Sing this as the Third Song.

1.

EXCEEDING faithful in thy word,
And just in all thy ways,
We do acknowledge thee, O Lord,
And therefore give thee praise;

For as thy promise thou didst pass,
Before thou went'st away,
Sent down thy Holy spirit was,
At his appointed day.

2.

While thy Disciples, in thy name,
Together did retire,
The Holy Ghost upon them came,
In cloven tongues of fire;
That in their calling they might be
Confirmed from above,
As thou wert, when he came on thee,
Descending like a dove.

3.

Whereby those men, that simple were,
And fearful till that hour,
Had knowledge at an instant there,
And boldness arm'd with power;
Receiving gifts so manifold,
That (since the world begun)
A wonder seldom hath been told,
That could exceed this one.

4.

Now also, blessed Spirit, come,
Unto our souls appear,

P

And of thy graces shower thou some
On this assembly here :
To us thy dove-like meekness lend
That humble we may be,
And on thy silver wings ascend,
Our Saviour Christ to see.

5.

Oh, let thy cloven tongues, we pray
So rest on us again,
That both the truth confess we may
And teach it other men.
Moreover, let thy heavenly fire,
Enflamed from above,
Burn up in us each vain desire,
And warm our hearts with love.

6.

Vouchsafe thou likewise to bestow
On us thy sacred peace,
We stronger may in Union grow,
And in debates decrease ;
Which peace, though many yet contemn,
Reformed let them be,
That we may (Lord), have part in them,
And they have part in thee.

TRINITY SUNDAY.

AFTER Arius, and other heretics, had broached their damnable fancies, whereby the faith of many, concerning the mystery of the blessed Trinity, was shaken, divers good men laboured in the rooting out of those pestilent opinions: and it was agreed upon by the Church, that some particular Sunday in the year should be dedicated to the memory of the Holy Trinity, and called Trinity Sunday, that the name might give the people occasion to enquire after the mystery. And moreover (that the pastor of each several congregation might be yearly remembered to treat thereof, as necessity required) certain portions of the Holy Scripture, proper to that end, were appointed to be read publickly that day. In some countries they observed this institution on the Sunday next before the Advent: and in other places the Sunday following Whitsunday, as in the Church of England.

SONG LIX.

Sing this as the Ninth Song.

1.

THOSE, oh, thrice holy Three in One,
  Who seek thy nature to explain,
By rules to human reason known,
Shall find their labour all in vain;
And in a shell they may intend
The sea, as well, to comprehend.

2.

What, therefore, no man can conceive,
Let us not curious be to know;
But, when thou bid'st us to believe,
Let us obey, let reason go:
Faith's objects true, and surer be,
Than those that reason's eyes do see.

8.

Yet, as by looking on the sun,
(Though to his substance we are blind,)
And by the course we see him run,
Some notions we of him may find:
So, what thy brightness doth conceal,
Thy word and works in part reveal.

OF THE CHURCH.

4.

Most glorious essence, we confess,
In thee (whom by our faith we view),
Three Persons, neither more or less,
Whose workings them distinctly shew:
And sure we are, those Persons three
Make but one God, and thou art he.

5.

The sun a motion hath, we know,
Which motion doth beget us light;
The heat proceedeth from those two,
And each doth proper acts delight:
The motion draws out time a line,
The heat doth warm, the light doth shine.

6.

Yet, though this motion, light, and heat,
Distinctly by themselves we take,
Each in the other hath his seat,
And but one sun we see they make:
For whatsoe'er the one will do,
He works it with the other two.

7.

So in the Godhead there is knit
A wondrous threefold true-love-knot,

And perfect union fastens it,
Though flesh and blood perceive it not;
And what each Person doth alone,
By all the Trinity is done.

8.

Their work they jointly do pursue,
Though they their offices divide;
And each one by himself hath due
His proper attributes beside:
But One in substance they are still,
In virtue one, and one in will.

9.

Eternal all the Persons be,
And yet Eternal there's but One;
So likewise Infinite all Three,
Yet infinite but One alone:
And neither Person aught doth miss,
That of the Godhead's essence is.

10.

In Unity and Trinity,
Thus, oh Creator, we adore
Thy ever-praised Deity,
And thee confess for evermore,
One Father, one begotten Son,
One Holy Ghost, in Godhead One.

SUNDAY IN GENERAL.

SUNDAY is our natural appellation, the Sabbath the Hebrew term, and the Lord's Day the Christian name, whereby we entitle God's Seventh Day; and (if wilful affectation be avoided) either name is allowable. It is a portion of time sanctified by God, immediately after the world's creation, and by the divine law dedicated to be perpetually observed to the honour of our creator: and though some things accidentally pertinent to the observation thereof have been changed, yet that which is essential thereunto is for ever immutable. Our Saviour hath by his Resurrection hallowed for us that which we now observe, instead of the Jewish Sabbath, which being the day whereon he rested in the grave, the observation thereof, and of all other Jewish ceremonies, was buried with him; because they were to continue but till the accomplishment of those things whereof they were types. This is that day wherein our Redeemer began (as it were) his eternal rest, after he had finished the work of our reparation, and conquered Death, the last that was to be destroyed. This day we ought, therefore, to sanctify, according to God's first institution: not Jewishly, that is, by a strict or mere outward abstaining from the servile works of the body only, according to the letter; but Christianity, to wit, in spirit and truth, both inwardly and outwardly; so recreating our bodies and souls, that we may, with a sanctified pleasure (and, as much as may be, without weariness) spend that day to the glory of God, according to his command, and the Church's direction; even to the use of bodily labours and exercises, whensoever (without respect to sensual or covetous ends) a rectified conscience shall persuade us, that the honour of God, the charity we owe to our neighbours, or an unfeigned necessity requires them to be done.

SONG LX.

Sing this as the Forty-fourth Song.

1.

SIX days, oh Lord, the world to make,
 And set all creatures in array,
Was all the leisure thou wouldst take,
And then didst rest the seventh day:
That day thou therefore hallowed hast,
And rightly, by a law divine,
(Which till the end of time shall last,)
The seventh part of time is thine.

2.

Then teach us willingly to give
 The tribute of our days to thee;
By whom we now both move and live,
And have attain'd to what we be,
For of that rest, which by thy word
Thou hast been pleased to enjoin,
The profit all is ours, oh Lord,
And but the praise alone is thine.

3.

Oh, therefore, let us not consent
To rob thee of thy Sabbath Day,
Nor rest with carnal rest content,
But sanctify it all we may;
Yea, grant that we from sinful strife,
And all those works thou dost detest;
May keep a Sabbath all our life,
 And enter thy eternal rest.

ST. ANDREW'S DAY.

THE holy Church celebrateth this day to glorify God for that favour which he vouchsafed unto her by the calling and ministry of blessed Andrew his Apostle; and that, by the remembrance of his readiness to follow and preach Christ, both the honourable and Christian memorial, due to an Apostle, might be preserved, and we stirred up also to the imitation of his forwardness in our several callings, advancing God's honour and gospel: in which general sense even the meanest Christian hath a kind of apostleship, to build up (not only in himself, but in others also) the temple of the living God, and to increase and establish the kingdom of Christ.

SONG LXI.

Sing this as the Forty-Fourth Song.

1.

AS blessed Andrew, on a day,
    By fishing did his living earn,
Christ came, and called him away,
That he to fish for men might learn:

OF THE CHURCH.

And no delay thereat he made,
Nor questions fram'd of his intent,
But quite forsaking all he had,
Along with him that call'd he went.

2.

Oh, that we could so ready be,
To follow Christ when he doth call!
And that we could forsake, as he,
Those nets that we are snar'd withal:
Or would this fisherman of men,
(Who set by all he had so light)
By his obedience shewed then
(And his example) win us might.

3.

But precepts and examples fail,
Till thou thy grace, Lord, add thereto;
O grant it, and we shall prevail
In whatsoe'er thou bid'st us do:
Yea, we shall then that bliss conceive,
Which in thy service we may find,
And for thy sake be glad to leave
Our nets, and all we have behind.

S. THOMAS'S DAY.

THIS day was set apart by the Church, that it might be sanctified to the praise of God for his holy Apostle St. Thomas, by whose preaching the Christian generation was multiplied; and that we might strengthen the belief we have of our Saviour's undeniable Resurrection, by taking a yearly occasion to refresh our memories with that part of the evangelical story, which mentioneth both this Apostle's doubting, and the confirmation of his faith by a sensible demonstration.

SONG LXII.

Sing this as the Ninth Song.

1.

WHEN Christ was risen from the dead,
    And Thomas of the same was told,
He would not credit it, he said,
Though he himself should him behold,
Till he his wounded hands had eyed,*
And thrust his fingers in his side.

* Seen.

2.

Which trial he did undertake,
And Christ his frailty did permit,
By his distrusting sure to make
Such others, as might doubt of it:
So we had right, and he no wrong,
For by his weakness both are strong.

3.

Oh, blessed God, how wise thou art!
And how confoundest thou thy foes!
Who their temptations dost convert,
To work those ends which they oppose:
When Satan seeks our faith to shake,
The firmer he the same doth make.

4.

Thus whatsoe'er he tempts us to,
His disadvantage let it be;
Yea, make those very sins we do,
The means to bring us nearer thee:
Yet let us not to ill consent,
Though colour'd with a good intent.

ST. STEPHEN'S DAY.

STEPHEN was one of the Seven Deacons mentioned Acts vi. and the first Martyr of Jesus Christ; whose truth having powerfully maintained by dispute, he constantly sealed it with his blood. The Church, therefore, hath appointed this anniversary in remembrance thereof, that so God might perpetually be glorified for the same; and the story of his martyrdom the oftener mentioned, to the encouragement and direction of other men in their trials.

SONG LXIII.

Sing this as the Fourth Song.

1.

LORD, with what zeal did thy first Martyr breathe
Thy blessed truth, to such as him withstood!
With what stout mind embraced he his death!
A holy witness sealing with his blood!
The praise is thine, that him so strong didst make,
And blest is he, that died for thy sake.

OF THE CHURCH.

2.

Unquenched love in him appeared to be
When for his murd'rous foes he did intreat ;
A piercing eye made bright by faith had he,
For he beheld thee in thy glory set ;
And so unmov'd his patience he did keep,
He died, as if he had but fallen asleep.

3.

Our lukewarm hearts with his hot zeal inflame,
So constant and so loving let us be !
So let us living glorify thy name :
So let us dying fix our eyes on thee ;
And when the sleep of death shall us o'ertake,
With him to life eternal us awake.

ST. JOHN THE EVANGELIST.

THIS day is celebrated by the Church to praise God for his blessed Evangelist and beloved Disciple, St. John, who hath been an admirable instrument of his glory, and the Church's instruction ; for the mystery of the sacred Trinity, and the Divinity of Christ, is by him most plainly expressed in his writings, among many other great mysteries and excellent doctrines concerning our redemption; for which we are bound particularly to honour God, and worthily stirred up thereunto by this annual commemoration.

SONG LXIV.

Sing this as the Forty-fourth Song.

1.

TEACH us by his example, Lord,
    For whom we honour thee to-day,
And grant his witness of thy Word
Thy church enlighten ever may :
And as beloved, oh Christ he was,
And therefore leaned on thy breast,
So let us also in thy grace,
And on thy sacred bosom rest.

2.

Into us breathe that life divine,
Whose testimony he intends :
About us cause thy light to shine,
That which no darkness comprehends :
And let that ever-blessed Word,
Which all things did create of nought,
Anew create us now, oh Lord,
Whose ruin sin hath almost wrought.

3.

Thy holy faith we do profess,
Us to thy fellowship receive;
Our sins we heartily confess,
Thy pardon therefore let us have;
And as to us thy servant gives
Occasion thus to honour thee,
So also let our words and lives
As lights and guides to others be.

INNOCENTS' DAY.

KING HEROD understanding that a King of the Jews was born in Bethlehem Juda (and fearing that by him he might be dispossessed), he murdered all the young infants of that circuit, in hope among them to have slain Jesus Christ: but he was sent into Egypt by God's special appointment; and so the tyrant's fury proved vain. In honour, therefore, of the Almighty's providence, the Church celebrateth this day; to put us in mind, also, how vainly the Devil and his members rage against God's decree: and, that the cruel slaughter of those poor infants may never be forgotten; which, in a large sense, may be called a Martyrdom; as in the generality of the cause (being for Christ), and in he passion of the body, though not in the intention of the mind: and so in proper sense doth St. Stephen hold still the place of the first captain of that band.

SONG LXV.

Sing this as the Forty-fourth Song.

1.

THAT rage, wherof the Psalm doth say,
 'Why are the Gentiles grown so mad?'
Appear'd in part upon that day,
When Herod slain the Infants had:
Yet (as it saith) they storm'd in vain,
(Though many Innocents they slew)
For Christ they purpos'd to have slain,
Who all their counsels overthrew.

2.

Thus still vouchsafe thou to restrain
All tyrants, Lord, pursuing thee;
Thus let our vast desires be slain,
That thou may'st living in us be;
So whilst we shall enjoy our breath,
We of thy love our songs will frame;
And, with those Innocents, our death
Shall also glorify thy name.

3.

In type those many died for one:
That one for many more was slain;
And what they felt in act alone,
He did in will and act sustain.
Lord, grant that what thou hast decreed,
In will and act we may fulfil;
And though we reach not to the deed,
From us, oh God, accept the will.

THE CONVERSION OF ST. PAUL.

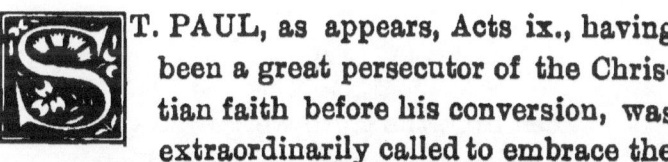T. PAUL, as appears, Acts ix., having been a great persecutor of the Christian faith before his conversion, was extraordinarily called to embrace the same profession, even as he proceeded in journey purposely undertaken to suppress the truth; and so, of a wolf became afterward a Pastor, and the most laborious Preacher of Jesus Christ; which mercy of God, that we may still remember it to the praise of his name, and our own comfort, the Church hath appointed a yearly commemoration thereof.

SONG LXVI.

Sing this as the Forty-fourth Song.

1.

A BLEST conversion and a strange,
Was that when Saul a Paul became,
And, Lord, for making such a change,
We praise and glorify thy name:
For whilst he went from place to place,
To persecute thy truth and thee,
(And running to perdition was)
By powerful grace called back was he.

2.

When from the truth we go astray,
(Or wrong it through our blinded zeal)
Oh come, and stop us in the way,
And then thy will to us reveal;
That brightness shew us from above,
Which proves the sensual eye-sight blind;
And from our eyes those scales remove,
That hinder us thy way to find.

8.

And as thy blessed servant Paul
When he a convert once became,

Exceeded thy Apostles all,
In painful preaching of thy name:
So grant that those who have in sin
Exceeded others heretofore,
The start of them in faith may win,
Love, serve, and honour thee tho more.

ST. MATTHIAS.

MATTHIAS was the Disciple which was chosen in the room of Judas Iscariot; and his anniversary is commanded to be observed, that it might give us continual occasion to praise God for his justice and favour; for his justice shewed in discovering and not sparing Judas the traitor, abusing his apostleship; for his favour declared in electing Matthias a faithful Pastor of the Church. Moreover, the remembrance of divers other mysteries is renewed by the observation of this day. And by taking occasion to read publickly the story of Judas's apostacy, men are that day put in mind to consider what judgments hang over their heads, who shall abuse the divine callings, etc.

SONG LXVII.

1.

WHEN one among the twelve there was,
   That did thy grace abuse,
Thou leftst him, Lord, and in his place
   Didst just Matthias choose:
So, if a traitor do remain
   Within thy church to-day,
To grant him true repentance deign,
   Or cast him out, we pray.

2.

Though horned like the lamb he shew,
   Or sheep-like clad he be,
Let us his dragon language know,
   And wolfish nature see;
Yea, cause the lot to fall on those,
   The charge of thine to take,
That shall their actions well dispose,
   And conscience of them make.

3.

Let us, moreover, mind his fall,
   Whose room Matthias got,
So to believe, and fear withal,
   That we forsake thee not:

For titles, be they ne'er so high,
Or great, or sacred place,
Can no man's person sanctify,
Without thy special grace.

ST. MARK'S DAY.

ST. MARK, being one of the four blessed Evangelists, by whose pen the Gospel of Jesus Christ was recorded; this day is purposely appointed to praise God for those glad tidings he brought, and that we might honour him also with such a Christian memorial, as becometh the Ambassador of so great a King as our Redeemer: which civil honour, due to the Saints of God, it is hoped none will deny them; nor conceive such institutions superstitious, or to have been purposed to an idolatrous end.

SONG LXVIII.

Sing this as the Forty-fourth Song.

1.

FOR those blest Penmen of thy Word,
    Who have thy holy Gospel writ,
We praise and honour thee, oh Lord,
And our belief we build on it:

Those happy tidings which it brings,
With joyful hearts we do embrace,
And prize, above all other things,
That precious token of thy grace.

2.

To purchase what we hope thereby,
Our utmost wealth we will bestow;
Yea, we our pleasures will deny,
And let our lives and honours go:
And whomsoe'er it cometh from,
No other Gospel we will hear;
No, though an Angel down should come
From heav'n, we would not give him ear.

3.

Our resolutions, Lord, are such,
But in performance weak are we;
And the deceiver's craft is much;
Our second, therefore, thou must be:
So we assuredly shall know,
When any doctrines we receive,
If they agreeing be, or no,
To those which we professed have.

ST. PHILIP AND JACOB.

THIS day is celebrated to the honour of God, and the Christian memorial of the two blessed Apostles, Philip and Jacob: at which time the Church taketh occasion to offer to our remembrance such mysteries, as Christ delivered unto them, that we might the oftener consider them, receive further instruction concerning them, and praise God, both for such his favours and for those instruments of his glory.

SONG LXIX.

Sing this as the Third Song.

1.

TO thy Apostles thou hast taught
  What they, oh Christ, should do;
And those things which believe they ought,
  Of thee they learned too:
And that which thou to them hast shewn,
  Hath been disposed thus,
They unto others made it known,
  And those have told it us.

2.

With them we do confess and say,
  (What shall not be denied)
Thou art the Truth, the Life, the Way,
  And we in thee will bide:
By thee the Father we have known,
  Whom thou descendest from;
And unto him, by thee alone,
  We have our hope to come.

3.

For thou to Philip didst impart,
  (Which our belief shall be)
That thou within the Father art,
  And that he is in thee;
And saidst, whatever in thy name
  We should with faith require,
Thou wouldst give ear unto the same,
  And grant us our desire.

4.

Of thee, oh Lord, we therefore crave,
  (Which thou wilt deign, we know)
The good belief which now we have
  We never may forego:
And that thy sacred truth, which we
  Thy Word have learned from,
From age to age deriv'd may be,
  Until thy kingdom come.

ST. BARNABAS'S DAY.

THIS day is solemnized in commemoration of St. Barnabas, a faithful Disciple of Jesus Christ; and to honour God for the benefit vouchsafed to the Church by his ministry; for he was a good man, full of the Holy Ghost, and of faith, as St. Luke testifieth, Acts xi., 24. He was also, by the Holy Ghost's immediate appointment (together with Paul) separated for the ministry of the Gospel, and confirmed in the Apostleship by the laying on of hands, Acts xiii., 2.

SONG LXX.

Sing this as the Forty-fourth Song.

1.

THY gifts and graces manifold,
    To many men thou, Lord, hast lent,
Both now, and in the days of old,
To teach them faith, and to repent:
Thy Prophets thou didst first ordain,
And they as legates did appear;

Then cams't thyself, and in thy train
Apostles for attendants were.

2.

For legier,* when thou went'st away,
The Holy Ghost thou didst appoint;
And here, successions, till this day,
Remain of those he did anoint;
Yea, thou hast likewise so ordain'd,
That to make good what those have taught,
An army royal was maintain'd
Of Martyrs, who thy battles fought.

3.

For those, and him, for whom we thus
Are met, to praise thy name to-day,
We give thee thanks, as they for us,
That should come after them, did pray
And by this duty we declare,
Our faith assures that they and we
(In times divided though we are)
Have one communion still with thee.

* Legacy.

ST. JOHN BAPTIST.

JOHN, called the Baptist, was he (as Christ himself testifieth) who was promised to be sent before him to prepare his way, Luke vii. 27, and by his preaching and baptism the people were accordingly prepared to receive him that was to follow. He was the true expected Elias, and slain by Herod, for reproving the incest which the said Herod committed, in taking his brother's wife. That we might praise God, therefore, for this Forerunner of our Saviour (and by his example remember to provide for his entertainment) the Church hath set apart this day.

SONG LXXI.

Sing this as the Ninth Song.

1.

BECAUSE the world might not pretend
It knew not of thy coming day,
Thou didst, oh Christ, before thee send
A cryer, to prepare thy way:
Thy kingdom was the bliss he brought,
Repentance was the way he taught.

2.

And, that his voice might not alone
Inform us what we should believe,
His life declar'd what must be done,
If thee we purpose to receive:
His life our pattern, therefore, make,
That we the course he took may take.

3.

Let us not gad to Pleasure's court,
With fruitless toys to feed the mind;
Nor to that wilderness resort,
Where reeds are shaken with the wind:
But tread the path he trod before,
That both a Prophet was, and more.

4.

Clad in repentant cloth of hair,
Let us, oh Christ, (to seek out thee)
To those forsaken walks repair,
Which of so few frequented be:
And true repentance so intend,
That we our courses may amend.

5.

Let us hereafter feed upon
The honey of thy Word divine;

OF THE CHURCH.

Let us the world's enticement shun,
Her drugs, and her bewitching wine;
And on our loins (so loose that are)
The leather-belt of temperance wear.

6.

Thus from the cryer let us learn,
For thee, sweet Jesus, to prepare,
And others of their sins to warn,
However for the same we fare:
So thou to us, and we to thee,
Shall when thou comest welcome be.

ST. PETER'S DAY.

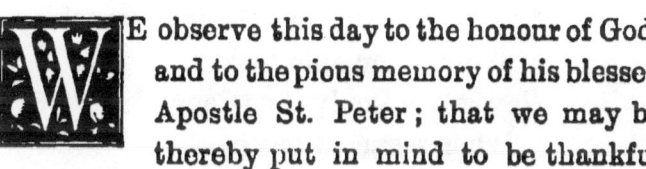E observe this day to the honour of God, and to the pious memory of his blessed Apostle St. Peter; that we may be thereby put in mind to be thankful for those continuing favours received by his ministry; that Pastors also may make him their pattern, in discharging the charge Christ committeth unto them; that by considering his weakness, we may all learn not to presume on our own strength; and that, by his Christian example, we may be taught to bewail our escapes with bitter tears of true repentance.

SONG LXXII.

Sing this as the Third Song.

1.

HOW watchful need we to become,
    And how devoutly pray,
That thee, oh Lord, we fall not from,
    Upon our trial day:
For, if thy great Apostle said,
    He would not thee deny,
Whom he that very night denayd,*
    On what shall we rely?

2.

For of ourselves we cannot leave
    One pleasure for thy sake;
No, not one virtuous thought conceive,
    Till us thou able make:
Nay, we not only thee deny,
    When persecutions be,
But, or forget, or from thee fly,
    When peace attends on thee.

3.

Oh! let those prayers us avail,
    Thou didst for Peter deign,

* Denied.

That when our foe shall us assail,
    His labour may be vain :
Yea, cast on us those powerful eyes,
    That mov'd him to lament,
We may bemoan, with bitter cries,
    Our follies, and repent.

4.

And grant that such as him succeed,
    For Pastors of thy fold,
Thy sheep and lambs may guide and feed,
    As thou appoint'st they should :
By his example speaking what
    They ought in truth to say,
And in their lives confirming that
    They teach them to obey.

ST. JAMES'S DAY.

THIS day we praise God for his blessed Apostle St. James, the son of Zebedeus, who was one of those two that desired of Christ they might sit at his right hand, and at his left, in his kingdom, as the Gospel for the day declareth; and by occasion of that ignorant petition (proceeding from their carnal weakness) Christ taught both them, and the rest of the Apostles, and all other Christians also, what greatness best becometh his followers; and that we are to taste the cup of his passion, before we can be glorified with him: so this holy Apostle did; for he was slain by Herod, as it is declared in the Epistle appointed for the day.

SONG LXXIII.

Sing this as the Forty-fourth Song.

1.

HE that his father had forsook,
    And followed Christ at his commands,
By human frailty overtook,
For place and vain preferment stands,
Till by his Master he was taught,
Of what he rather should have care,
How undiscreetly he had sought,
And what his servant's honours are.

2.

Whereby we find how much ado
The best men have this world to leave;
How, when they wealth and friends forego,
Ambitious aims to them will cleave:

And sure this angel-sin aspires
In such men chiefly to reside,
That have "put off" those brute desires,
Which in the vulgar sort abide.

3.

To thee, oh God, we therefore pray,
Thy humble mind may in us dwell;
And charm that fiend of pride away,
Which would thy graces quite expel:
But, of all other, those men keep
From this delusion of the foe,
Who are the Shepherds of thy sheep,
And should each good example show.

4.

For such as still pursuing be
That greatness which the world respects,
Their servile baseness neither see,
Nor feel thy Spirit's rare effects:
And doubtless they, who most of all
Descend to serve both thee and thine,
Are those, who in thy kingdom shall
In seats of greatest glory shine.

ST. BARTHOLOMEW.

THIS day is consecrated to the honour of God, and the pious memory of his blessed Apostle St. Bartholomew, that (as appeareth in the Epistle appointed for the day) we might take occasion to praise our Redeemer for those many wonders which were wrought by his Apostles, to the great increase of the Christian faith, and open confusion of the Church's adversaries.

SONG LXXIV.

Sing this as the Ninth Song.

1.

EXCEEDING gracious favours, Lord,
 To thy Apostles hast thou shown;
And many wonders by thy Word,
And in thy name, by them were done:
The blind did see, the dumb could talk,
The deaf did hear, the lame did walk.

OF THE CHURCH.

2.

They all diseases took away:
The dead to life they did restore;
Foul spirits dispossessed they,
And preached the gospel to the poor:
The Church grew strong, thy faith grew plain,
Their foes grew mad and mad in vain.

3.

Oh! let their works forever be
In honour to thy gloriours name;
And by thy power vouchsafe that we
(Whom sin makes deaf, blind, dumb, and lame)
May hear thy word, and see thy light,
And speak thy truth and walk aright.

4.

Each deadly sickness of the soul,
Let thy Apostles' doctrines cure:
Let them expel the spirits foul,
Which make us loathsome and impure,
That we the life of faith may gain
Who long time dead in sin hath lain.

ST. MATTHEW.

S T. MATTHEW, otherwise called LEVI, was a publican, that is, a custom-gatherer; from which course of life (being hateful in those countries) he was called to the Apostleship, and became also one of the four Evangelists; to his religious memory, therefore, and to honour God, for the favour vouchsafed (both to him and us) by his ministry this day is observed by the Church's authority.

SONG LXXV.

Sing this as the Forty-fourth Song.

1.

WHY should unchristian censures pass
    On men, or that which they profess?
A publican St. Matthew was,
Yet God's beloved ne'ertheless:
And was elected one of Christ's
Apostles and Evangelists;

2.

For God doth not a whit respect
Profession, person, or degree;
But maketh choice of his elect
From every sort of men that be,
That none might of his love despair,
But all men unto him repair.

3.

For those, oh let us therefore pray,
Who seem uncalled to remain;
Not shunning them, as cast away,
God's favour never to obtain:
For some awhile neglected are,
To stir in us more loving care.

4.

And for ourselves, let us desire,
That we our avarice may shun,
When God our service shall require,
As this Evangelist hath done,
And spend the remnant of our days
In setting forth our Maker's praise.

ST. MICHAEL AND ALL ANGELS.

THIS day we glorify God for the victory of St. Michael and his angels obtained over the Dragon and his angels; whereby the Church is freed from being prevailed against by the furious attempts or malicious accusations of the Devil. This commemoration is apointed, also, to mind us thankfully to acknowledge God's mercy towards us, in the daily ministry of his Angels, who are said to pitch their tents about his children, and to defend them from the temptations and mischievous practices of evil spirits, watching every moment for advantage to destroy them: which, if we oftener considered, and how there be armies of Angels and Devils, night and day, fighting for us, and round about us, we would become more careful how we grieved those good Spirits (who attend us for our safety), to the rejoicing of them that seek our destruction. By St. Michael, who was Prince of the good Angels (and termed by St. Jude an Archangel), some understood Jesus Christ; for he is indeed the principal Messenger or Angel of our salvation, and the chief of the Princes, as holy Daniel called him; yea, to him alone this name Michael (which signifieth *who is like God*) doth most properly appertain, seeing he only is the perfect image of his Father.

SONG LXXVI.

Sing this as the Forty-fourth Song.

1.

TO praise, oh God, and honour thee,
  For all thy glorious triumphs won,
Assembled here this day are we,
And to declare thy favours done:
Thou took'st that great Archangel's part,
With whom in Heaven the Dragon fought;
And that good army's friend thou wert,
That cast him and his angels out.

2.

Whereby we now in safety are,
Our dangers all secured from;
For to increase thy glory here,
Thy kingdom with great power is come:
And we need stand in dread no more,
Of that enraged fiend's despite,
Who in thy presence, heretofore,
Accused us both day and night.

3.

In honour of thy blessed name,
This hymn of thanks we therefore sing;

And to thine everlasting fame,
Through Heav'n thine endless praise shall ring:
We praise thee for thy proper might,
And, Lord, for all those Angels too,
Who in thy battles came to fight,
Or have been sent thy will to do.

4.

For many of that glorious troop,
To bring us messages from thee,
From Heav'n vouchsafed have to stoop,
And clad in human shape to be:
Yea, we believe they watch and ward
About our persons evermore,
From evil spirits us to guard:
And we return thee praise therefore.

ST. LUKE.

THIS day we memorize the benefit the Church received by the blessed Evangelist St. Luke, a physician both for soul and body, and the first ecclesiastical historiographer; for he was author, not only of that Gospel, which beareth his name; but also of that book called the Acts of the Apostles,

OF THE CHURCH.

and an eye-witness of most part of that which he hath written, remaining a constant companion of St. Paul in his tribulations: worthily, therefore, ought we to honour him with a Christian memorial and praise God for the grace vouchsafed us by his means.

SONG LXXVII.

Sing this as the Forty-fourth Song.

1.

IF those physicians honour'd be,
   That do the body's health procure,
Then worthy double praise is he,
Who can both soul and body cure.
In lifetime both ways Luke excell'd,
And those receipts hath also left,
Which many soul-sick patients heal'd,
Since from the world he was bereft.

2.

And to his honour this beside,
A blessed witness hath declar'd,
That constant he did still abide,
When others from the truth were scar'd:
For which the glory, Lord, be thine,
For of thy grace those gifts had he,

And thou his actions didst incline,
Our profit, and his good, to be.

3.

By his example, therefore, Lord,
Uphold us, that we fall not from
The true profession of thy Word,
Nor by this world be overcome;
And let his wholesome doctrine heal
That leprous sickness of the soul,
Which more and more would on her steal,
And make her languish and grow foul.

SIMON AND JUDE, APOSTLES.

THIS day is dedicated to the praise of God, and the pious memory of the two blessed Apostles of Jesus Christ, Simon called Zelotes, or the Canaanite, and Jude the brother of James. And in this solemnity we are, among other things, principally put in mind of that love, which Christ commandeth to be continued among us, and of that heed we ought to have unto our abiding in that state of grace, whereunto God hath called us, as appeareth in the Epistle and Gospel appointed for the day.

SONG LXXVIII.

Sing this as the Third Song.

1.

NO outward mark we have to know
  Who thine, oh Christ, may be,
Until a Christian love doth show
  Who appertains to thee :
For knowledge may be reach'd unto,
  And formal justice gain'd,
But till each other love we do,
  Both faith and works are feign'd.

2.

Love is the sum of those commands,
  Which thou with thine dost leave ;
And for a mark on them it stands,
  Which never can deceive :
For when our knowledge folly turns,
  When shows no shew retain,
And zeal itself to nothing burns,
  Then love shall still remain.

3.

By this we thy Apostles knit,
  And joined so in one,

Their true-love-knot could never yet
  Be broken, nor undone :
Oh let us, Lord, received be
  Into that sacred knot,
And one become, with them and thee,
  That sin undo us not.

4.

Yea, lest when we thy grace possess,
  We fall again away,
Or turn it into wantonness,
  Assist thou us, we pray :
And, that we may the better find
  What heed there should be learn'd,
Let us the fall of Angels mind,
  As blessed Jude hath warn'd.

ALL SAINTS' DAY.

THIS day the Church hath appointed, that, to the praise of God, and our comfort, we should commemorate that excellent mystery of the Communion of Saints (which is one of the twelve articles of Christian belief) : and that (considering how admirably the divine wisdom hath knit all his

OF THE CHURCH. 255

elect into one body, for their more perfect enjoying both of his love, and the love of one another) we might here receive a taste of the pleasure we shall have in the full fruition of that felicity, and be stirred up also to such mutual love and unity, as ought to be betwixt us in this life. This is the last Saint's Day in the ecclesiastic circuit of the year, generally observable by the ancient ordinance of the Church; and it seemeth to have a mystery in it, shewing that when the circle of time is come about, we shall, in one everlasting holy day, honour that blessed communion and mystical body, which shall be made perfect, when all those (whom we have memorised apart) are united into one: that is, when the Father, the Son, the Holy Ghost, the Angels, and all the holy Elect of God, shall be incorporated together into a joyful, unspeakable and inseparable union in the kingdom of Heaven: which the Almighty hasten, Amen.

SONG LXXIX.

Sing this as the Ninth Song.

1.

NO bliss can so contenting prove,
   As universal love to gain,

Could we with full requiting love
All men's affections entertain;
But such a love the heart of man
Nor weil contain, nor merit can.

2.

For though to all we might be dear,
(Which cannot in this life befal)
We discontented should appear,
Because we had not hearts for all:
That we might all men love, as we
Beloved would of all men be.

3.

For love in loving joys as much,
As love for loving to obtain;
Yea love unfeigned is likewise such,
It cannot part itself in twain:
The rival's friendship soon is gone,
And love divided loveth none.

4.

Which causeth that with passions pain'd
So many men on earth we see;
And had not God a means ordain'd,
This discontent in heaven would be;
For all the saints would jealous prove
Of God's and of each other's love.

5.

But he whose wisdom hath contriv'd
His glory, with their full contents,
Hath rom himself to them deriv'd
This favour (which that strife prevents).
One body all his saints he makes,
And for his spouse this one he takes.

6.

So each one of them shall obtain
Full love from all, returning to
Full love to all of them again,
As members of one body do:
None jealous, but all striving how
Most love to others to allow.

7.

For as the soul is all in all,
And all through every member too,
Love in that body mystical
Is as the soul, and fills it so ;
Uniting them to God as near
As to each other they are dear.

8.

Yea, what they want to entertain,
Such overflowing love as his,

He will supply, and likewise deign
What for his full delight they miss;
That he may all his love employ,
And they return his fill of joy.

9.

The seed of this content was sown,
When God the spacious world did frame,
And ever since the same hath grown,
To be an honour to his name;
And when his Saints are sealed all,
This mystery unseal he shall.

10.

Meanwhile as we in landscape view
Fields, rivers, cities, woods, and seas,
And (though but little they can shew),
Do therewithal our fancies please,
Let contemplation maps contrive
To shew us where we shall arrive.

11.

And though our hearts too shallow be,
That blest communion to conceive,
Of which we shall in Heaven be free,
Let us on earth together cleave:
For those who keep in union here,
Shall know by faith what will be there.

12.

Where all those Angels we admir'd,
With every Saint since time begun,
(Whose sight and love we have desir'd),
Shall be with us conjoin'd in one:
And we and they, and they and we,
To God himself espoused be.

13.

Oh happy wedding! where the guests,
The bride and bridegroom shall be one;
Where songs, embraces, triumphs, feasts,
And joys and love are never done:
But thrice accurst are those that miss
Their garment when this wedding is.

14.

Sweet Jesus, seal'd and clad, therefore,
For that great meeting let us be,
(Where people, tongues, and kindreds, more
Than can be told, attend on thee),
To make those shouts of joy and praise,
Which to thine honour they shall raise.

ROGATION WEEK.

THIS is called *Rogation Week*, being so termed by antiquity *a rogando*, from the public supplications; for then the Litany, which is full of humble petitions and intreaties, was, with solemn procession, usually repeated; because there be, about that season, most occasions of public prayer, in regard princes go then forth to battle; the fruits and hope of plenty are in their blossom; the air is most subject to contagious infections; and there is most labouring and travelling, both by land, and sea also, from that time of the year forward. Which laudable custom (though it be lately much decayed, and in some countries abused from the right end, and mingled with superstitious ceremonies) is in many places orderly retained, according as the Church of England approveth it; and we yearly make use also of those processions, to keep knowledge of the true bounds of our several parishes, for avoiding of strife. And those perambulations were yearly appointed likewise, that, viewing God's yearly blessing upon the grass, the corn, and other fruits of the earth, we might be the more provoked to praise him.

SONG LXXX.

Sing this as the Forty-fourth Song.

1.

IT was thy pleasure, Lord, to say,
   That whatsoever in thy name
We pray'd for, as we ought to pray,
Thou wouldst vouchsafe to grant the same:
Oh, therefore, we beseech thee now,
To these our prayers which we make,
Thy gracious ear in favour bow,
And grant them for thy mercy's sake.

2.

Let not the seasons of this year,
(As they their courses do observe),
Engender those contagions here,
Which our transgressions do deserve:
Let not the summer worms impair
Those bloomings of the earth we see;
Nor blastings, or distemper'd air,
Destroy those fruits that hopeful be.

3.

Domestic brawls expel thou far,
And be thou pleas'd our coast to guard;

The dreadful sounds of in-brought war
Within our confines be not heard :
Continue also here thy Word,
And make us thankful (we thee pray);
The pestilence, dearth, and the sword,
Have been so long withheld away.

4.

And, as we heedfully observe
The certain limits of our grounds,
And outward quiet to preserve,
About them walk our yearly rounds :
So let us also have a care,
Our soul's possessions, Lord, to know,
That no encroachments on us there
Be gained by our subtle foe.

.5.

What pleasant groves, what goodly fields!
How fruitful hills and dales have we !
How sweet an air our climate yields !
How stor'd with flocks and herds are we !
How milk and honey doth o'erflow !
How clear and wholesome are our springs !
How safe from ravenous beasts we go !
And oh, how free from poisonous things !

6.

For these, and for our grass, our corn;
For all that springs from blade or bough;
For all those blessings that adorn
Or wood, or field, this kingdom through:
For all of these, thy praise we sing,
And humbly (Lord), entreat thee too.
That fruit to thee we forth may bring,
As unto us thy creatures do.

7.

So in the sweet refreshing shade
Of thy protection sitting down,
Those gracious favours we have had,
Relate we will to thy renown;
Yea, other men, when we are gone,
Shall for thy mercies honour thee,
And famous make what thou hast done,
To such as after them shall be.

ST. GEORGE'S DAY.

THIS may be called the Court Holiday; for with us it is solemnized upon command in the court royal of the Majesty of Great Britain only, or in the families of those Knights of the Order, who are constrained to be absent from the solemnity there held, which is usually on the day anciently dedicated to George the Martyr. Nevertheless, we believe not that it was he whom they anciently chose to be the Patron of the forenamed order; for the relation of him who delivered the lady from the dragon is only a Christian allegory, invented to set forth the better the Church's deliverance. Jesus Christ is the true St. George, and our English tutelary Saint; even he that cometh armed upon the White Horse, Rev. xix. 11. The Dragon he overthrows is the Beast mentioned in the same chapter, and called (a little before) 'the Dragon with seven heads and ten horns': the lady he delivers is that woman whom the Dragon persecutes, Rev. xii. And to the honour of him I conceive the most honourable order of St. George to be continued, and this day consecrated. Nor is there any irreverence in imposing this name on our Redeemer; for George signifieth a Husbandman, which is a name or attribute that even Christ applied to his Father, John xv. 2. 'My Father,' saith he, (ὁ Γεωργὸς ἐστι) ' is the George,' or the Husbandman. And, indeed, very properly may this nation call GOD their George or Husbandman, or he hath (as it were) moted this island with the sea, walled it with natural bulwarks, built towers in it, planted his truth here, weeded, dressed, and replenished it like a garden: and, in a word, every way done the part of a good Husbandman thereon. Howsoever, therefore, the first occasion of this day's great solemnity seem but mean (as the beginning of many noble inventions were) yet I conceive that institution to have been ordained to weighty and Christian purposes: even to oblige the Peers of this kingdom, by the new and strict bands of an honourable order, to imitate their Patron's care over his vineyard, to remember them, that they are the band-royal, to whom the guard thereof is committed, to stir up in them virtuous emulations, and to shew them how to make use of their temporal dignities to the glory of God. For, beside many other reverend officers, there belongs a Prelate also to these solemnities; and, methinks, we should not imagine that the Founder of it (being a Christian Prince, assisted by a wise and religious counsel) would have so profaned the most excellent dignity of the Church, as to make it wait on ceremonies ordained for ostentation or some other vain ends. More discreetly they deal, who apprehend the contrary, and are not in danger of this sentence, 'Evil to him that evil thinketh.'

SONG LXXXI.

Sing this as the Third Song.

1.

ALL praise and glory that we may,
    Ascribe we Lord, to thee,
From whom the triumphs of this day,
    And all our glories be:
For of itself, nor east, nor west,
    Doth honour ebb or flow,
But as to thee it seemeth best,
    Preferments to bestow.

2.

Thou art, oh Christ, that valiant Knight,
    Whose order we profess,
And that Saint George, who oft doth fight
    For England in distress:
The Dragon thou o'erthrew'st is he,
    That would thy Church devour,
And that fair Lady, (Lord), is she,
    Thou savest from his power.

3.

Thou like a Husbandman prepar'd
   Our fields yea sown them hast;
And, Knight-like, with a warlike guard.
   From spoil enclosed them fast.
Oh deign that those who in a band
   More strict than heretofore,
Are for this vineyard bound to stand,
   May watch it now the more:

4.

Yea grant since they elected are,
   New orders to put on,
And sacerd hieroglyphics wear,
   Of thy great conquest won,
That those, (when they forget,) may tell
   Why such of them are worn,
And inwardly inform as well,
   As outwardly adorn;

5.

That so their Christian Knighthood may,
   No Pagan order seem:
Nor they their meetings pass away,
   As things of vain esteem;
And that we may our triumphs all
   To thy renown apply,
Who art that Saint, on whom we call,
   When we Saint George do cry.

FOR PUBLIC DELIVERANCES.

GOD hath vouchsafed unto this kingdom many public deliverances, which ought never to be forgotten, but rather should be celebrated by us, as the days Purin by the Israelites, Hester ix. 26. Especially that of the fifth of November: for the celebration whereof there is a statute enacted; and it is hoped we shall never neglect or be ashamed to praise God for that delivery, according to provision made to that purpose. For that, and the like occasions, therefore, this Hymn is composed.

SONG LXXXII.

Sing this as the Ninth Song.

1.

WITH Israel we may truly say,
    If on our side God had not been,
Our foes had made of us their prey,
And we this light had never seen :
The pit was digg'd, the snare was laid,
And we with ease had been betray'd.

OF THE CHURCH.

2.

But they that hate us undertook
A plot they could not bring to pass;
For he that all doth overlook,
Prevented what intended was:
We found the pit, and 'scap'd the gin,*
And saw their makers caught therein.

3.

The means of help was not our own,
But from the Lord alone it came;
(A favour undeserved shown);
And therefore let us praise his name:
Oh, praise his name, for it was he
That broke the net, and set us free,

4.

Unto his honour let us sing,
And stories of his mercy tell;
With praises let our temples ring,
And on our lips thanksgiving dwell:
Yea, let us not his love forget,
While sun or moon doth rise or set.

5.

Let us redeem again the times,
Let us begin to live anew,

* Snare

And not revive those heinous crimes,
That dangers past so near us drew;
Lest he that did his hand revoke,
Return it with a double stroke.

6.

A true repentance takes delight
To mind God's favours heretofore;
So, when his mercies men recite,
It makes a true repentance more:
And where those virtues do increase,
They are the certain signs of peace.

7.

But where increasing sins we see,
And to such dulness men are grown,
That slighted those protections be,
Which God in former time hath shown,
It shall betoken to that land
Some desolation near at hand.

8.

Our hearts, oh, never harden so,
Nor let thine anger so return:
But with desire thy will to do,
For our offences let us mourn:
And mind to praise (e'en tears among),
Thy mercies in a joyful song.

FOR THE COMMUNION.

WE have a custom among us, that, during the time of administering the blessed Sacrament of the Lord's Supper, there is some Psalm or Hymn sung, the better to keep the thoughts of the Communicants from wandering after vain objects: this Song, therefore (expressing a true thankfulness, together with what ought to be our faith concerning that mystery, in such manner as the vulgar capacity may be capable thereof) is offered up to their devotion, who shall please to receive it.

SONG LXXXIII.

Sing this as the Third Song.

1.

THAT favour, Lord, which of thy grace
    We do receive to-day,
Is greater than our merit was,
    And more than praise we may:

For, of all things that can be told,
  That which least comfort hath,
Is more than e'er deserve we could,
  Except it were by wrath.

2.

Yet we not only have obtain'd
  This world's best gifts of thee,
But thou thy flesh hast also deign'd
  Our food of life to be;
For which, since we no mends can make,
  (And thou requir'st no more)
The cup of saving health we take,
  And praise thy name therefore.

3.

Oh teach us rightly to receive
  What thou dost here bestow;
And learn us truly to conceive,
  What we are bound to know;
That such as cannot wade the deep
  Of thy unfathom'd Word,
May, by thy grace, safe courses keep
  Along the shallow ford.

4.

This mystery, we must confess,
  Our reach doth far exceed

And some of our weak faiths are less
   Than grains of mustard seed :
Oh, therefore, Lord, increase it so,
   We fruit may bear to thee,
And that implicit faith may grow
   Explicit faith to be.

5.

With hands we see not as with eyes;
   Eyes think not as the heart;
But each retains what doth suffice
   To act his proper part :
And in the body, while it bides,
   The meanest member shares
That bliss, which to the best betides,
   And as the same it fares.

6.

So, if in union unto thee
   United we remain,
The faith of those that stronger be,
   The weaker shall sustain :
Our Christian love shall that supply,
   Which we in knowledge miss,
And humble thoughts shall mount us high,
   E'en to eternal bliss.

                                                  T

7.

Oh, pardon all those heinous crimes,
    Whereof we guilty are :
To serve thee more in future times,
    Our hearts do thou prepare ;
And make thou gracious in thy sight
    Both us, and this we do,
That thou therein mayst take delight,
    And we have love thereto.

8.

No new oblation we devise,
    For sins preferr'd to be ;
Propitiatory sacrifice
    Was made at full by thee :
The sacrifice of thanks is that,
    And all that thou dost crave,
And we ourselves are part of what
    We sacrificed have.

9.

We do no gross realities
    Of flesh in this conceive :
Or that their proper qualities
    The bread or wine do leave :
Yet in this holy Eucharist
    We, (by a means divine,)

Know we are fed with thee, oh Christ,
   Receiving bread and wine.

10.

And though the outward elements
   For signs acknowleg'd be,
We cannot say thy Sacraments
   Things only signal be:
Because, whoe'er thereof partakes,
   In those this power it hath,
It either them thy members makes,
   Or slaves of sin and death.

11.

Nor unto those do we incline,
   (But from them are estrang'd),
Who yield the form of bread and wine,
   Yet think the substance chang'd:
For we believe each element
   Is what it seems indeed,
Although that in thy Sacrament
   Therewith on thee we feed.

12.

Thy real presence we avow,
   And know it so divine,
That carnal reason knows not how
   That presence to define:

For when thy flesh we feed on thus,
   (Though strange it do appear),
Both we in thee, and thou in us,
   E'en at one instant are.

13.

No marvel many troubled were,
   This secret to unfold,
For mysteries faith's objects are,
   Not things at pleasure told.
And he that would by reason sound,
   What faith's deep reach conceives,
May both himself and them confound,
   To whom his rules he leaves.

14.

Let us, therefore, our faith erect
   On what thy Word doth say,
And hold their knowledge in suspect,
   That new foundations lay:
For such full many a grievous rent
   Within thy Church have left;
And by thy peaceful Sacrament
   The world of peace bereft.

15.

Yea, what thy pledge and seal of love
   Was first ordain'd to be,

Doth great and hateful quarrels move
    Where wrangling spirits be :
And many men have lost their blood
    (Who did thy name profess),
Because they hardly understood
    What others would express.

16.

Oh, let us not hereafter so,
    About mere words contend,
The while our crafty common foe
    Procures on us his end :
But if in essence we agree,
    Let all with love essay
A help unto the weak to be,
    And for each other pray.

17.

Love is that blessed cement, Lord,
    Which must us reunite ;
In bitter speeches, fire and sword,
    It never took delight :
The weapons those of malice are,
    And they themselves beguile,
Who dream that such ordained were
    Thy Church to reconcile.

18.

Love brought us hither, and that love
    Persuades us to implore,
That thou all Christians hearts wouldst move
    To seek it more and more;
And that self-will no more bewitch
    Our minds with foul debate,
Nor fill us with that malice which
    Disturbs a quiet state.

19.

But this especially we crave,
    That perfect peace may be
'Mong those that disagrèed have
    In show of love to thee;
That they with us, and we with them,
    May Christian peace retain,
And both in New Jerusalem
    With thee for ever reign.

20.

No longer let ambitious ends,
    Blind zeal, or cankered spite,
Those Churches keep from being friends,
    Whom love should fast unite:
But let thy glory shine among
    Those candlesticks, we pray,

OF THE CHURCH. 279

We may behold what hath so long
   Exil'd thy peace away:

21.

That those, who, heeding not thy word,
   Expect an earthly power,
And vainly think some temporal sword
   Shall Antichrist devour;
That those may know thy weapons are
   No such as they do feign,
And that it is no carnal war
   Which we must entertain.

22.

Confessors, Martyrs, Preachers strike
   The blows that gain this field:
Thanks, prayer, instructions, and the like,
   Those weapons are they wield:
Long-suffering, patience, prudent care,
   Must be the court-of-guard;
And faith and innocency are
   Instead of walls prepar'd.

23.

For these (no question), may as well
   Great Babel overthrow,
As Jericho's large bulwarks fell,
   When men did ram's-horns blow;

Which, could we credit, we should cease
    All bloody plots to lay,
And to suppose God's holy peace
    Should come the Devil's way.

24.

Lord, let that flesh and blood of thine,
    Which fed us hath to-day,
Our hearts to thy true-love incline,
    And drive ill thoughts away:
Let us remember what thou hast
    For our mere love endur'd,
E'en when of us despis'd thou wast,
    And we thy death procur'd.

25.

And with each other, for thy sake,
    So truly let us bear,
Our patience may us dearer make,
    When reconcil'd we are:
So when our courses finish'd be,
    We shall ascend above
Sun, moon, and stars, to live with thee,
    That art the God of Love.

EMBER WEEK.

THE Ember Weeks are four fasts, anciently solemnized at the four principal seasons of the year, and by an institution appointed to be observed for divers good purposes. First, to humble ourselves by fasting and prayer, that God might, upon our humiliation, be moved to grant us the blessings belonging to those seasons. Secondly, that it might please God to strengthen our constitutions against the distemperatures occasioned by the several humours predominate at those times, to the endangering of our bodily healths. Thirdly, that we might be remembered to dedicate a part of every season to God's glory. And lastly, that there might be a public fasting and prayers made for those (according to the Apostle's use) who by the laying on of hands were to be confirmed in the ministry of the Gospel: for the Sunday next after these fasts is the time ordinarily appointed for the ordination of such as are called to those offices.

SONG LXXXIV.

Sing this as the Ninth Song.

1.

THOU dost, from ev'ry season, Lord,
To profit us, advantage take,
And at their fittest times afford
Thy blessings for thy mercy's sake:
At winter, summer, fall, or spring,
We furnish'd are of ev'ry thing.

2.

A part, therefore, from each of these,
With one consent reserv'd have we,
In prayer and fasting to appease
That wrath our sins have mov'd in thee;
And that thou mayst not, for our crimes,
Destroy the blessings of the times.

3.

Oh, grant that our devotions may
With true sincereness be perform'd,
And that our lives, not for a day,
But may for ever be reform'd:
Lest we remain as fast in sin,
As if we ne'er had fasting been.

4.

Our constitutions temper so,
Those humours, which this season reign,
May not have power to overthrow
That health which yet we do retain :
Else, through that weakness which it brings,
Lord, make us strong in better things.

5.

And, since thy holy Church appoints
These times, thy workmen forth to send,
And those for Pastors now annoints,
Who on thy fold are to attend :
Bless thou, where they who (should ordain)
With prayer and fasting hands have lain.

6.

Oh, bless them, ever blessed Lord,
Whom for thy work the Church doth choose;
Instruct them by thy sacred Word,
And with thy Spirit them infuse,
That live and teach aright they may,
And we their teaching well obey.

These that follow are Thanksgivings for Public Benefits.

FOR SEASONABLE WEATHER.

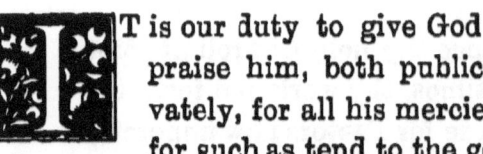T is our duty to give God thanks, and praise him, both publickly and privately, for all his mercies; especially for such as tend to the general good: and, therefore, the Church hath in her Liturgy ordained set forms of Thanksgiving for such ends; in imitation whereof these following Hymns are composed, that we might the oftener, and with more delight exercise this duty, which is most properly done in song: and thereby, also, the forms of Thanksgiving are much the more easily learned of the common people, to be sung of them amid their labours. This, that next follows, is a Thanksgiving for seasonable Weather; by means whereof we enjoying the blessings of the earth, ought at all times to praise God for the same.

SONG LXXXV.

Sing this as the Third Song.

1.

LORD, should the sun, the clouds the wind,
    The air, and seasons be
To us so froward and unkind,
    As we are false to thee;
All fruits would quite away be burn'd,
    Or lie in water drown'd,
Or blasted be, or overturn'd,
    Or chilled on the ground.

2.

But, from our duty though we swerve,
    Thou still dost mercy show,
And deign thy creatures to preserve,
    That men might thankful grow;
Yea, though from day to day we sin,
    And thy displeasure gain,
No sooner we to cry begin,
    But pity we obtain.

3.

The weather now thou changed hast,
    That put us late to fear,

And when our hopes were almost past,
   Then comfort did appear.
The Heaven the earth's complaint hath heard,
   They reconciled be,
And thou such weather hast prepar'd,
   As we desir'd of thee:

4.

For which, with lifted hands and eyes,
   To thee we do repay
The due, and willing sacrifice
   Of giving thanks to day;
Because such offerings we should not
   To render thee be slow;
Nor let that mercy be forgot,
   Which thou art pleas'd to show.

FOR PLENTY.

PLENTY is the cure of famine, and a blessing which, above all other, we labour and travail for; yet when we have obtained the same, it makes us many times so wanton, instead of being thankful, that we forget not only God's mercy in that, but abuse all other benefits. To put us, therefore, in mind of our duty, and to express the better a continual thankfulness to the Almighty, this Hymn is composed.

SONG LXXXVI.

Sing this as the Third Song.

1.

HOW oft, and in how many crimes,
   Thee jealous have we made;
And, blessed God, how many times
   Have we forgiveness had?
If we with tears to bed at night
   For our transgressions go,
To us thou dost, by morning light,
   Some comfort deign to show.

2.

This pleasant land, which for our sin
   Was lately barren made,
Her fruitfulness doth new begin,
   And we are therefore glad:
We for those creatures thankful be,
   Which thou bestowest, Lord,
And for that plenty honour thee,
   Which thou dost now afford.

3.

Oh, let us therewith in excess
　Not wallow, like to swine,
Nor into graceless wantonness
　Convert this grace of thine;
But so revive our feeble powers,
　And so refresh the poor,
That thou mayst crown this land of ours
　With plenties evermore.

FOR PEACE.

PEACE is the nurse of Plenty, and the means of so many other blessings, both public and private, that God can never be sufficiently praised for it; yet, instead of glorifying him, men most commonly abuse it to the dishonour of God, and their ruin. This Hymn, therefore, is composed, that it may give occasion to us more often to meditate God's mercy, and to glorify his name, who, above all other nations, have tasted the sweetness of this benefit.

SONG LXXXVII.

Sing this as the Third Song.

1.

SO cause us, Lord, to think upon
    Those blessings we possess,
That what is for our safety done,
    We truly may confess:
For we, whose fields, in time forepast,
    Most bloody war did stain,
Whilst fire and sword doth others waste,
    In safety now remain.

2.

No armed troops the ploughman fears:
    No shot our walls o'erturn;
No temple shakes about our ears;
    No village here doth burn:
No father hears his pretty child
    In vain for succour cry;
Nor husband sees his wife defil d,
    Whilst he half dead doth lie.|

3.

Dear God, vouchsafe to pity those,
    In this distress that be;

They, to protect them from their foes,
  May have a friend of thee:
For, by thy friendship we obtain
  These gladsome peaceful days,
And, (somewhat to return again,)
  We thus do sing thy praise.

4.

We praise thee for that inward peace,
  And for that outward rest,
Wherewith, unto our joy's increase,
  This kingdom thou hast blest:
Oh, never take the same away,
  But let it still endure:
And grant, oh Lord, it make us may
  More thankful, not secure.

FOR VICTORY.

OUR God is the Lord of Hosts, and the God of Battles: whensover, therefore, we have gotten the upper hand over our enemies, we ought not to glory in our own strength, policy, or value, but to ascribe the glory of it to him only, and return him public thanks for making us victorious over our enemies: and this Hymn serveth to help their devotion, who are willing to perform that duty.

SONG LXXXVIII.

Sing this as the Forty-fourth Song.

1.

WE love thee, Lord, we praise thy name,
　　Who, by thy great Almighty arm,
Hast kept us from the spoil and shame
Of those, that sought our causeless harm :
Thou art our life, our triumphs-song,
The joy and comfort of our heart;
To thee all praises do belong,
And thou the Lord of Armies art.

2.

We must confess it is thy power
That made us masters of the field;
Thou art our bulwark and our tower,
Our rock of refuge, and our shield;
Thou taughtst our hands and arms to fight;]
With vigour thou didst gird us round;
Thou mad'st our foes to take their flight,
And thou didst beat them to the ground.

3.

With fury came our armed foes,
To blood and slaughter fiercely bent,

And perils round us did enclose,
By whatsoever way we went;
That hadst thou not our Captain been,
(To lead us on, and off again),
We on the place had dead been seen,
Or mask'd in blood and wounds had lain.

4.

This Song we therefore sing to thee,
And pray that thou for evermore
Wouldst our Protector deign to be,
And at this time, and heretofore:
That thy continual favour shown,
May cause us more to thee incline,
And make it through the world be known,
That such as are our foes are thine.

FOR DELIVERANCE FROM A PUBLIC SICKNESS.

THE Pestilence, and other public sicknesses, are those arrows of the Almighty, wherewith he punisheth public transgressions: this Hymn, therefore, is to praise him, when he shall unslack the bow which was bent against us; and the longer he withholds his hand, the more constantly ought we to continue our public thanksgivings; for when we forget to persevere in praising God for his mercies past, we usually revive those sins that will renew his judgments.

SONG LXXXIX.

Sing this as the Ninth Song.

1.

WHEN thou would'st Lord, afflict a land,
  Or scourge thy people that offend,
To put in practice thy command,
Thy creatures all on thee attend;
And thou, to execute thy word,
Hast famine, sickness, fire, and sword.

2.

And here among us, for our sin,
A sore disease hath lately reign'd,
Whose fury so unstay'd hath been,
It could by nothing be restrain'd,
But overthrew both weak and strong,
And took away both old and young.

3.

To thee our cries we therefore sent,
Thy wonted pity, Lord, to prove;

Our wicked ways we did repent,
Thy visitation to remove;
And thou thine Angel didst command,
To stay his wrath-inflicting hand.

4.

For which thy love, in thankful wise,
Both hearts and hands to thee we raise,
And in the stead of former cries,
Do sing thee now a Song of Praise;
By whom the favour yet we have
To 'scape the never filled grave.

FOR THE KING'S DAY.

THE first day of Kings' Reigns hath been anciently observed in most kingdoms; and with us that custom is worthily retained, partly for civil ends, and partly that the people might assemble together, to praise God for the benefit the commonwealth receiveth by the Prince; to pray for his preservation also; and to desire a blessing upon him and his government; to which purpose this Song is composed.

SONG XC.

Sing this as the Third Song.

1.

WHEN, Lord, we call to mind those things,
    That should be sought of thee,
Remembering that the hearts of Kings
    At thy disposing be ;
And how, of all those blessings which
    Are outwardly possest,
To make a kingdom safe and rich,
    Good Princes are the best ;

2.

We thus are mov'd to sing thy praise
    For him thou deigned hast,
And humbly beg, that all our days
    Thy care of us may last.
Oh, bless our King, and let him reign
    In peaceful safety long,
The Faith's Defender to remain,
    And shield the truth from wrong.

3.

With awful love, and loving dread,
    Let us observe him, Lord ;
And, as the members with their head,
    In Christian peace accord :

And fill him with such royal care,
  To cherish us for this,
As if his heart did feel we are
  Some living parts of his.

4.

Let neither party struggle from
  That duty should be shown,
Lest each to other plagues become,
  And both be overthrown:
For, o'er a disobedient land
  Thou dost a tyrant set,
And those, that tyrant-like command
  Have still with rebels met.

5.

Oh, never let so sad a doom
  Upon these kingdoms fall;
And to assure it may not come,'
  Our sins forgive us all:
Yea, let the parties innocent
  Some damage rather share,
Than, by unchristian discontent,
  A double curse to bear.

6.

Make us, (that placed are below,
  Our callings to apply),

Not over curious be to know
  What he intends on high;
But teach him justly to command,
  Us rightly to obey,
So both shall safe together stand,
  And doubts shall fly away.

7.

When hearts of Kings we pry into,
  Our own we do beguile;
And what we ought ourselves to do,
  We leave undone the while;
Whereas, if each man would attend
  The way he hath to live,
And all the rest to thee commend,
  Then all should better thrive.

8.

Oh, make us, Lord, disposed thus,
  And our dread Sovereign save;
Bless us in him, and him in us,
  We both may blessings have;
That many years for him we may
  This Song devoutly sing,
And mark it for a happy day,
  When he became our King.

HERE ENDETH THE HYMNS AND SONGS OF THE CHURCH.

THE AUTHOR'S HYMN.

GREAT Almighty, God of Heaven!
Honour, praise, and glory be
Now, and still hereafter given,
For thy blessings deigned me;
Who hast granted and prepared
More than can be well declared.

By thy mercy thou didst raise me
From below the pits of clay;
Thou hast taught my lips to praise thee,
Where thy love confess I may;
And those blessed hopes dost leave me,
Whereof no man can bereave me.

By thy grace, those passions, troubles,
And those wants that me opprest,
Have appear'd as water-bubbles,
Or as dreams, and things in jest;
For thy (leisure still attending,)
I with pleasure saw their ending.

Those afflictions, and those terrors,
Which to others grim appear.
Did but shew me where my errors
And my imperfections were:
But distrustful could not make me
Of thy love, nor fright nor shake me.

When in public to defame me,
A design was brought to pass,
On their heads, that meant to shame me,
Their own malice turned was;
And that day, most grace was shown me,
Which they thought should have undone me.*

Therefore, as thy blessed Psalmist,
When he saw his wars had end,
(And his days were at the calmest,)
Psalms and Hymns of praises penn'd:
So my rest by thee enjoyed,
To thy praise I have employed.

Yea, remembering what I vowed,
When enclos'd from all but thee,
I thy presence was allowed,
While the world neglected me:

---

* This stanza is not in the Edition of 1623. It was added in the later editions.

This my Muse hath took upon her,
That she might advance thine honour.

Lord, accept my poor endeavour,
And assist thy servant so,
In good studies to persever,
That more fruitful he may grow;
And become thereby the meeker,
Not his own vain glory seeker.

Grant my frailties and my folly,
(And those daily sins I do,)
May not make this work unholy,
Nor a blemish bring thereto:
But, let all my faults committed
With compassion be remitted.

Those base hopes that would possess me,
And those thoughts of vain repute,
Which do now and then oppress me,
Do not, Lord, to me impute;
And though part they will not from me,
Let them never overcome me.

Till this present, from obsceneness,
Thou, oh Lord, hast kept my pen;
And my verse abhorr'd uncleanness,
Though it vain were, now and then:

My loose thoughts it ne'er inflamed,
But I thereby them have tamed.

Still withhold me from delighting
That, which thine may misbeseem;
And from every kind of writing,
Whereby this may lose esteem;
That I may with faith and reason,
Every future volume season.

Oh, preserve me from committing
Aught that's heinously amiss;
From all speeches him unfitting,
That hath been employ'd on this:
Yea, as much as may be deigned,
Keep my very thoughts unstained.

That these helps unto devotion
May no scandal have at all,
Lord, I make to thee this motion,
For their sakes that use them shall:
Of the world I am not fearful,
Nor of mine own glory careful.

Whilst thy favours thou dost deign me,
I despise the world's respect;
And most comfort entertain me,
When I suffer most neglect:

Yea, I then am best rewarded,
When I seem the least regarded.

For, (oh,) when I mind my Saviour,
And how many a spiteful tongue
Slander'd his most pure behaviour,
And his pious't works did wrong:
I contented am, and care not,
Though my life detraction spare not.

Therefore, when that I shall blamed,
Or with cause, or causeless be,
So thy truth be not defamed,
Fall what can befall on me:
Let my fame of none be friended,
So thy Saints be not offended.

That is most my fear, (oh Father;)
Thy assistance therefore lend;
And, oh let me perish rather,
Than thy little ones offend:
Let my life some honour do thee,
Or by death return me to thee.

For thy praise I wish and love it;
And, (oh,) let my end be shame,
If for mine own sake I covet
Either life, or death, or fame:

So it may be to thy glory,
Let detraction write my story.

But to thee which way availing,
Can my shame or honour be?
Truth shall ever be prevailing,
Whatsoe'er is thought of me:
Thou nought loseth through my folly,
Nor gain'st aught by the most holy.

And, I know, that whatsoever
Hath thy glory in esteem,
Will accept this good endeavour,
Whatsoe'er the workman seem;
Let, (oh therefore) be fulfilled
That which thou, oh Lord, hast willed.

And when I, with Israel's Singer,
To these Songs of Faith shall learn
Thy ten-stringed law to finger,
And that music to discern;
Lift me to that angel quire,
Whereunto thy Saints aspire!

THE END.

TO THE READER.

THAT such as have skill, and are delighted with music, may have the more variety, to stir up the soon cloyed affections, these Hymns are fitted with many new tunes; nevertheless, all (but some few of them) may be sung to such tunes as have been heretofore in use. For the benefit, therefore, of those who have no experience in music, I have here set down which songs they be, and to what old tunes they may be sung.

To the tune of the 1, 2, 3, and of an hundred other Psalms, may be sung Songs 3, 21, 32, 33, 35, 38, 43, 53, 57, 58, 67, 69, 72, 78, 81, 83, 85, 86, 87, 90.

To the tune of the 51, 100, 125 Psalms, and the Ten Commandments, &c., may be sung Songs 5, 6, 8, 11, 12, 27, 28, 34, 42, 44, 48, 51, 52, 56, 60, 61, 64, 65, 66, 68, 70, 73, 76, 77, 80, 88.

To the tune of the 112, 127 Psalms, and the Lord's Prayer, &c., may be sung Songs 7, 40, 41, 45, 49, 50, 54, 59, 62, 71, 74, 75, 79, 82, 84, 89.

To the tune of the 113 Psalm may be sung Songs 9, 10, 17.

To the tune of the 25 Psalm may be sung Song 20.

To the tune of the 124 Psalm may be sung Song 47.

Printed by W. REEVES, 185, Fleet Street, London, E.C.

THE TUNES TO WITHER'S SONGS.
COMPOSED BY ORLANDO GIBBONS.

Song 4. (p. 23.)

Song 5. (p. 26.)

Wither's Songs.

Song 9. (p. 41.)

Song 13. (p. 53.)

Song 31. (p. 133.)

Wither's Songs.] (6)

Song 34. (p. 144.)

Song 44. (p. 168.)

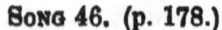

Song 46. (p. 178.)

Song 67. (p. 230.)

Wither's Songs.]   FINIS.

www.ingramcontent.com/pod-product-compliance
Lightning Source LLC
Chambersburg PA
CBHW020225240426
43672CB00006B/418